WINNING CHESS EXERCISES FOR KIDS

WINNING CHESS EXERCISES FOR KIDS

TACTICS AND STRATEGIES TO OUTSMART YOUR OPPONENT

VIKTORIA NI

Z KIDS • NEW YORK

TO MY MOTHER, WHO TAUGHT ME HOW TO PLAY CHESS AND
TRAVELED WITH ME TO TOURNAMENTS ALL AROUND THE WORLD.

AND TO MY FAMILY, WHO NEVER STOPPED BELIEVING IN ME.

Published in the United States by Z Kids, an imprint of Zeitgeist™,

a division of Penguin Random House LLC, New York.

zeitgeistpublishing.com

Zeitgeist™ is a trademark of Penguin Random House LLC

ISBN: 9780593690390

Ebook ISBN: 9780593689912

Illustrations by Foxy Fox, Tartila, Babich Alexander, and Vapart/Shutterstock.com

Book design by Emma Hall

Diagrams by Stalions Design

Author photograph © by Polina Viluna

Edited by Ada Fung

Printed in the United States of America

1st Printing

CONTENTS

INTRODUCTION

Welcome to the exciting world of chess! My name is Viktoria. I am an international master in chess who's been playing and loving chess for 25 years. For the past 13 years, I've been a chess teacher, so I'm thrilled to be your guide in this book!

Chess is a game that has captured the hearts and minds of countless people throughout history and around the world. I've represented the US and Latvian national women's teams, which gave me the opportunity to travel to more than 80 countries and live on three different continents. To me, one of the most beautiful things about chess is that it's a common global language: once you learn, you can play with anyone, anywhere in the world, without being able to speak one word to each other!

This book will help you defeat challenging opponents, whether you're casually playing against your friends or competing in chess tournaments. You'll learn moves, tactics, and strategies that strengthen your game and make you a better player.

This book will also let you put that knowledge into practice with plenty of chess exercises. These exercises will help you develop your pattern recognition, strategic thinking, planning, and problem-solving—all skills that will benefit you in chess, as well as many other areas of your life.

Some exercises will be challenging, but don't give up! Chess requires a lot of patience and practice, and the more you play and study, the more you'll improve. Other exercises may seem easy for you, but do them anyway! They will help reinforce the fundamentals of the game.

Finally, have fun! I'm excited to help you become a better chess player, and I can't wait to see where your chess journey takes you—who knows, maybe we'll compete one day!

HOW TO READ THE DIAGRAMS

Before we begin, let's break down how to read the diagrams in this book. Some diagrams are designed from the perspective of the white player, while others are designed from the perspective of the black player.

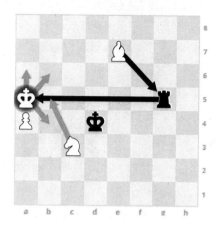

DIAGRAM A: Playing from the white perspective

As you can see in diagram A, on a board from the white perspective, the vertical columns, which are called files, go from a (at the left) to h (at the right), and the horizontal rows, which are called ranks, go from 1 (at the bottom) to 8 (at the top). The board is flipped in the black perspective (diagram B), so the files will go from h (at the left) to a (at the right), and the ranks will go from 8 (at the bottom) to 1 (at the top).

In the exercises, a white number 1 or black number 2 will show you which color you are playing as.

Some diagrams will have annotations that show you what's happening. Here's what they mean:

DIAGRAM B: Playing from the black perspective

GREEN ARROW: A move or capture

BLACK ARROW: A threat or attack

GREEN HIGHLIGHT: Shows the spot a piece moved from

BLACK HIGHLIGHT: The king in check

CIRCLES: Highlighting pieces or spaces on the board

CHAPTER 1

KNOW THE BOARD, KNOW THE PIECES

This chapter is a beginner's guide to chess. You'll learn the name, movement, role, and value of each chess piece and how the pieces work together on the board. We'll discuss how to set up the board, and you'll learn some fun historical facts along the way.

SETTING UP THE BOARD

A chessboard is a square divided into 64 squares of alternating colors—usually black and white. The chessboard is positioned so each player has a white square in the right-hand corner closest to them.

White moves first, and each player takes turns moving one piece at a time.

Each player has 16 pieces: eight pawns; two knights, bishops, and rooks; and one queen and king. Each piece has a point value, which tells us how important and valuable it is compared to the other pieces.

DIAGRAM 1.1: Ranks and files

Diagram 1.1 shows the starting placement of chess pieces. As you can see, the pawns begin on the "front lines," in ranks (rows) 2 and 7, with the more valuable pieces behind them, in ranks (rows) 1 and 8.

CHESS NOTATION

Chess players use a special code, called notation, to communicate and record their games. Versions of this secret language have existed for hundreds of years, so it even lets us study games played in the 1800s! Many chess games are written about in notation; it's the fastest and most efficient way to record a game. A general understanding of chess notation will help you understand the answer key in this book.

Here's how it works:

- Each square on the chessboard has a name with two parts: a letter (representing the file/column) and a number (representing the rank/row). In diagram 1.2, square d3 is in the fourth column from the white player's left and the third square up.
- Most pieces have a one-letter code, often the first letter in their name: K for king, Q for queen, B for bishop, and R for rook. Because the K is taken, knights are shortened to N. The lowly pawn doesn't have a letter.
- To describe a move, combine the letter for the piece you moved with the square you moved it to. If you moved your queen to f6, you would write Qf6. If you moved your knight to b7, you would write Nb7. Since pawns don't have letters, a pawn moved to b4 is just written as b4.
- If you capture a piece, place an x between the code letter and square name. So, if the queen captured a piece on f6, you would write Qxf6.
- If a move you make checks the king, you would add a + at the end. So, if moving the queen to f6 checks the king, you would write Qf6+.

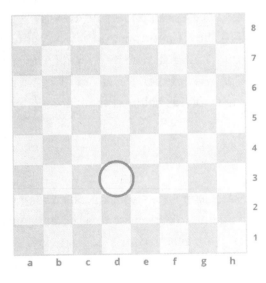

DIAGRAM 1.2: Square d3

THE PAWN

Pawns are the smallest pieces on the chessboard. Located in the front rows (ranks 2 and 7), they're usually the first to be moved. They may seem unimportant, but when they work together they can be a mighty force.

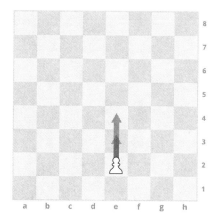

DIAGRAM 1.3: Pawn's movement

POINT VALUE: 1 point

MOVEMENT: Pawns move forward one square at a time, except on their first move, when they can move two squares (see diagram 1.3).

CAPTURE: Pawns capture other pieces diagonally, one row/rank ahead. Pawns also have a special capture move called en passant that we'll cover in chapter 5.

STRENGTHS

- There are a lot of them, so they take up space and prevent movement of opposing pieces.
- Pawns in the center of the board control the center—a good strategy.
- They can provide support and safe squares for friendly pieces.
- They can provide a protective barrier for the king.
- When a pawn reaches the last row/rank on the opposite side of the board (8 for white and 1 for black), it can be promoted to any same-color piece except a king. This is called **pawn promotion** (see page 64).

WEAKNESSES

- They can't move backward and may restrict the movement of friendly pieces.
- They can often be easily attacked and captured.

THE BISHOP

The **bishop** looks like a bishop's hat. Each player starts with two bishops on their side—one on a white square and one on a black square, in columns/files c and f.

POINT VALUE: 3 points

MOVEMENT: The bishop moves diagonally any number of squares in a straight line, along the same color squares as its starting square.

CAPTURE: The bishop can capture any of the opponent's pieces in its path and take its place.

DIAGRAM 1.4: Bishop's movement

STRENGTHS

- When positioned in or near the center, the bishop can cover a lot of space on the board.
- It is good at attacking pieces at the edges of the board and in corners.

WEAKNESSES

- It can only travel diagonally.
- If the bishop is trapped in a corner or blocked in, it can be difficult to move it.

THE KNIGHT

Knights often look like a horse's head. Each player starts the game with two knights, positioned in columns/files b and g.

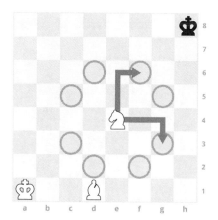

DIAGRAM 1.5: Knight's L-shaped movement (it can land on any of the circles)

POINT VALUE: 3 points

MOVEMENT: The knight moves in a unique L-shape, ending on a different-colored square than the one it started on. It can move two squares across and one up or down, or one square across and two up or down (see diagram 1.5). It's the only piece that can jump over other pieces.

CAPTURE: A knight can only capture an opponent's piece if it lands on the square where that piece is located, not if it jumps over it.

STRENGTHS

- Because it can jump over other pieces, the knight can reach squares that other pieces can't.
- The knight's unique movement can be difficult to predict.

WEAKNESSES

- Because of its unique movement, it can be difficult for beginners to use effectively.
- They can only move a short distance compared to some other pieces.
- When near an edge or corner, its movement and attack abilities are limited.
- They are often less useful near the endgame, with fewer pieces on the board.

THE ROOK

The **rook** looks like a little castle. Each player starts with two rooks in opposite corners of their side. The rook is the second-most powerful piece, after the queen. Generally, rooks are among the last pieces to be moved into action.

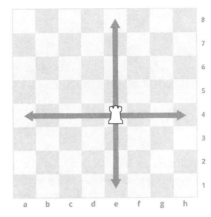

DIAGRAM 1.6: Rook's movement

POINT VALUE: 5 points

MOVEMENT: The rook can move any number of squares horizontally or vertically.

CAPTURE: The rook can capture any opponent's piece in its path.

STRENGTHS

- It can move a long distance, which is great for attacking or protecting.
- It can control important areas of the board, especially when in the middle.
- It is excellent at protecting multiple pieces at once.

WEAKNESSES

- It isn't good at attacking pieces on the edge or in corners, because it can't move diagonally.
- Other pieces, like the knight or bishop, can sneak up on the rook and capture it if it's not protected.
- Rooks start the game in the corner and can get blocked in by other pieces.

THE QUEEN

The **queen**, the most powerful piece, is tall with a pointed crown. The white queen starts the game on the white square nearest the center of the last row, and the black queen begins on the black square nearest the center of the last row.

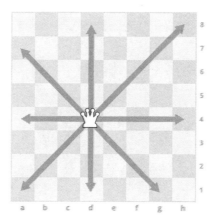

DIAGRAM 1.7: Queen's movement

POINT VALUE: 9 points

MOVEMENT: The queen can move vertically, horizontally, or diagonally any number of squares.

CAPTURE: The queen can capture any opponent's piece in its path.

STRENGTHS
- It can attack or defend almost anywhere on the board.
- It is a major piece in many tactical ideas and checkmate patterns.

WEAKNESSES
- It can be overused or engaged too early, leaving her trapped or vulnerable.
- Losing the queen usually leads to losing the game.

THE KING

The **king** is the most important—and most vulnerable—piece. This tallest piece has a rounded crown with a cross on top. The king starts at the center of the last row, next to the queen. Once your king is in **check**, meaning attacked and in danger, you must move it to safety or block the check. If a king cannot escape check, it is in **checkmate**—attacked with no escape—and the game ends.

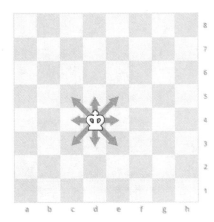

DIAGRAM 1.8:
King's movement

POINT VALUE: Infinity

MOVEMENT: Kings can only move one square in any direction: vertically, horizontally, or diagonally. Kings cannot move into check or directly next to the opponent's king.

CAPTURE: Kings can capture any piece except for the opponent's king.

STRENGTHS:
- It can move in any direction.
- It can castle with a rook, which helps protect it (more on this later).
- In the endgame, the king becomes more active and can help support other pieces.

WEAKNESSES:
- It can only move one square at a time.
- Opponents work hard to attack it.

YOUR TURN!

Now let's test your understanding of the different chess pieces!

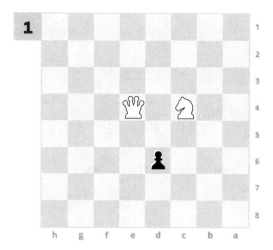

1

Which square(s) can the pawn move to?

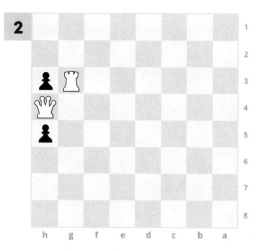

2

Can either of the pawns capture a white piece?

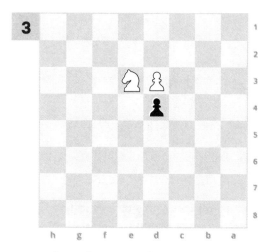

3

What piece can the pawn capture?

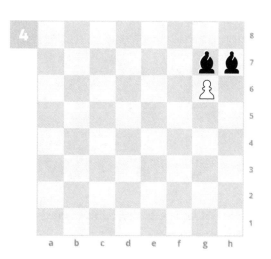

4

What piece can the pawn capture?

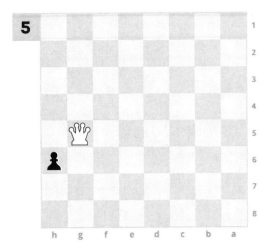

5

How many moves will it take to promote the pawn?

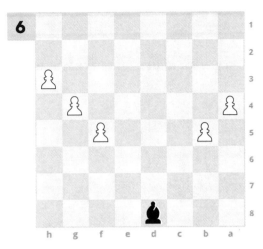

6

Which squares can the bishop move to?

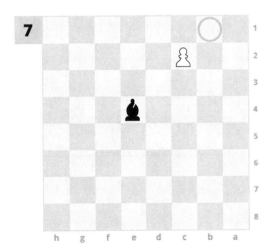

7

True or False: The bishop can move to b1 in one move.

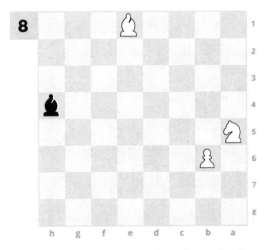

8

Capture all the white pieces in the fewest moves possible, assuming they don't move.

9

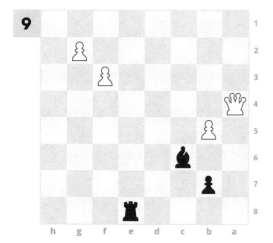

List all the squares the bishop can move to without being captured.

10

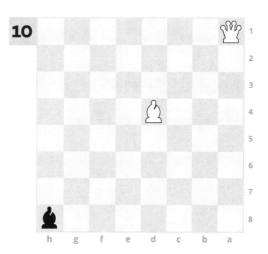

True or False: Your bishop can capture the white queen in one move.

11

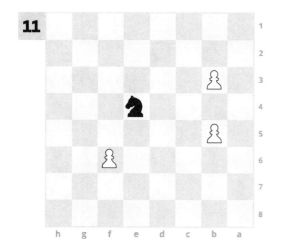

Which pawn(s) can your knight capture?

A. all the pawns

B. pawn on b3

C. pawn on f6

12

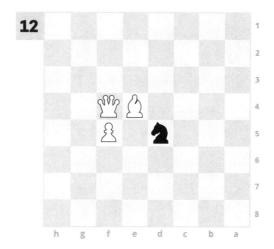

True or False: Your knight can capture the pawn and queen with one move.

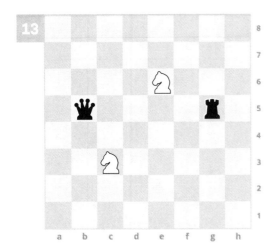

13

Using both knights, capture the queen and the rook in two moves, assuming they don't move.

14

Which four pieces can your knight capture back-to-back and in what order?

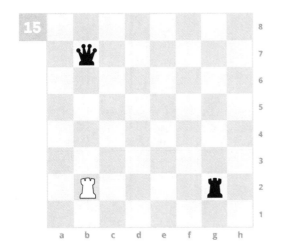

15

True or False: Your rook can capture either piece.

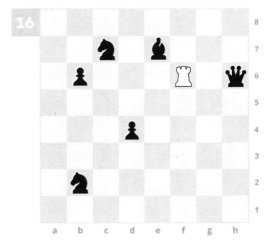

16

List all the pieces the rook can capture with one move.

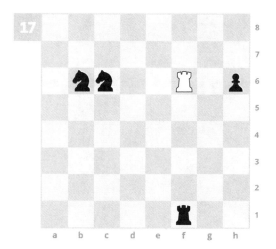

Which is the best piece for your rook to capture?

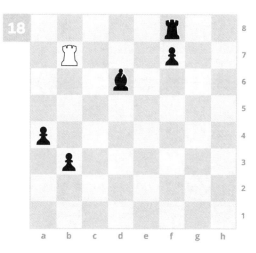

List all the squares your rook can move to without being captured.

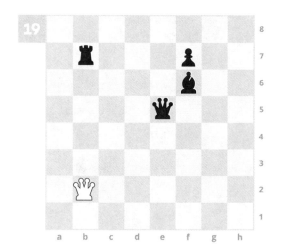

Which is the best piece for your queen to capture?

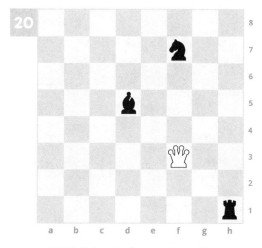

Which is the best piece for your queen to capture?

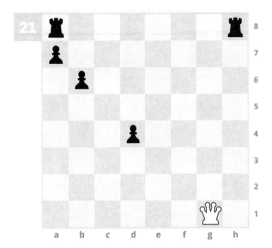

Find the shortest way(s) to capture all the black pieces, assuming they don't move.

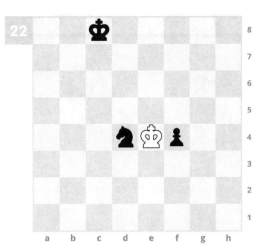

Which piece should your king capture?

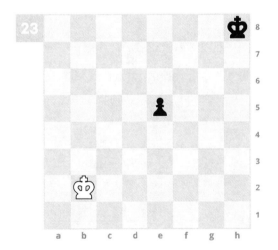

How many moves will it take your king to capture the pawn?

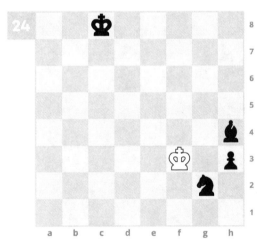

Find the shortest way to capture all the black pieces except the king.

CHAPTER 2

BASIC RULES AND PRINCIPLES

Now that we've explored the different chess pieces, let's focus on the game itself! In this chapter, we'll go over some of the basic rules of chess, including fair play, the three stages of the game, how to gain material advantage, when to exchange—and when not to.

BE A GOOD SPORT

Games, including chess, are meant to be enjoyable, and fair play is a big part of that. We all want to play with someone who's pleasant to be with! Some fair-play tips include:

- Shake hands before and after the game.
- Be gracious in victory and defeat. Always congratulate your opponent on a good game.
- Don't distract your opponent during the game.
- Don't tease your opponent or criticize their moves.
- When watching another game, don't make loud noises or otherwise distract the players.

LOSING IS A LEARNING OPPORTUNITY

Losing is never easy, but it's part of learning. Even the best chess players have lost many games throughout their careers. When we lose, it can be tempting to feel upset or discouraged. But I learn more from the games I lose than the games I win! By taking the time to understand why you lost, you can figure out where you can improve your strategy and become a better player.

UNDERSTANDING THE THREE PHASES

A chess game is divided into three phases: the opening, the middle game, and the endgame. The goal of the **opening** is to control the center of the board and **develop** your pieces. This means getting pieces out from starting positions into more active squares where they can attack and defend.

The **middle game** is typically the longest phase. You'll use your developed pieces to attack and defend. You can create weaknesses in your opponent's position and take advantage of them. You can also try to create strong pawn structures and control important squares on the board—especially in the center.

In the **endgame**, there are only a few pieces left on the board, and the goal is to either checkmate your opponent's king or promote your pawns. Not every game will reach the endgame; many games reach checkmate in the opening or middle game stage.

Typically, the player who wins the game gets one point; the player who loses gets zero points. If a game ends in a draw, each player gets half a point.

Good play in the opening can set you up for triumph in the middle and endgame. And errors in the opening or middle game can lead to a tough endgame, so it's important to always play carefully and think ahead.

CONTROL THE MIDDLE

The **center** is made up of the four squares in the middle of the board (see diagram 2.1). By using your first moves to control these squares, you can control more of the board and create more opportunities for your pieces. One way is to advance the two center pawns forward two squares. Another option is to move your knights to two of the four central squares.

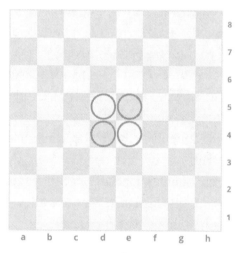

DIAGRAM 2.1: The center

KEEP YOUR KING SAFE!

It is crucial to keep your king away from the opponent's attacking pieces (typically pawns, bishops, and knights). To keep your king safe, castle your king or shelter it behind a wall of pawns and pieces as soon as possible (we'll explore how in chapter 3). Avoid leaving your king in the middle of the board or undefended. In diagram 2.2, the black king is safely away from the center files, sheltered behind a wall of pawns, a knight, and a rook. Meanwhile, the white king is at risk, near the center and behind the player's most valuable piece (the queen).

DEVELOP YOUR PIECES QUICKLY

In the opening phase, you want to develop your pieces, or move them into more active squares to attack and defend. One general rule is to develop all your pieces before moving them again—unless you have a good reason to do so, like capturing an undefended piece. Another general rule is always to move knights before bishops because knights can be developed more easily in the opening moves. Since they move in a unique L-shaped way, this allows them to influence central squares.

When you develop your pieces quickly, you can:

DIAGRAM 2.2: Black's king is well protected

DIAGRAM 2.3: White is developed

- control the center of the board
- build a strong, coordinated formation
- protect your king by creating a defensive barrier
- create threats and opportunities to attack or gain advantages

In diagram 2.3, you can see that the white pieces are developed and ready to play. Plus, they control two of the center squares and have protected their king. This is a good start!

Let's practice the three opening principles!

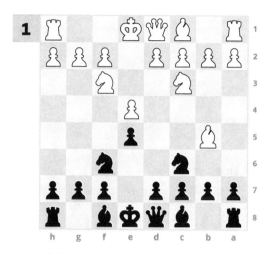

Pick the best move.

A. Bishop to c5

B. Pawn to d6

C. Pawn to h6

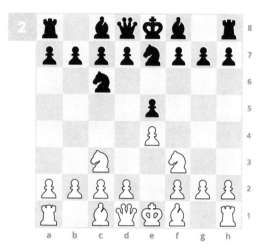

Pick the best move.

A. Bishop to d3

B. Bishop to c4

C. Knight to g5

Pick the best move.

A. Pawn to b3

B. Pawn to d3

C. Pawn to d4

Pick the best move.

A. Bishop to b4

B. Knight to c6

C. Knight to f6

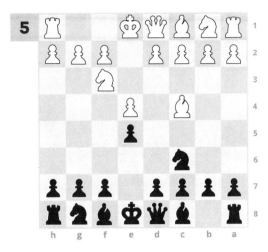

Pick the best move.

A. Knight on g8 to e7

B. Bishop to c5

C. Knight on c6 to e7

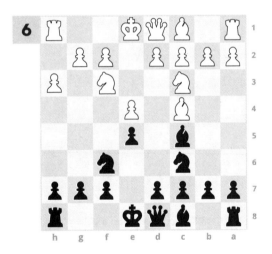

Pick the best move.

A. Knight captures pawn on e4

B. Pawn to d5

C. Pawn to d6

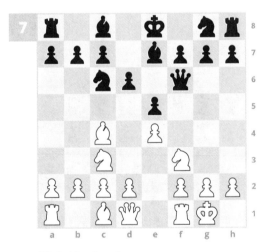

Pick the best move.

A. Pawn to h3

B. Knight to d5

C. Pawn to d3

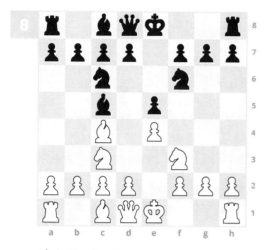

Pick the best move.

- A. Bishop to d5
- B. Knight to g5
- C. Pawn to d3

True or False: White is better developed.

True or False: The best move to protect the knight on e4 is pawn to f3.

True or False: Black should move pawn to g6 next.

True or False: White should capture the knight on c6.

True or False: You should move pawn to f6 to defend the pawn on e5.

True or False: White has better control of the center.

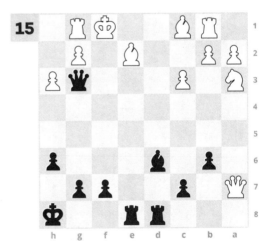

True or False: Your king is more protected than the white king.

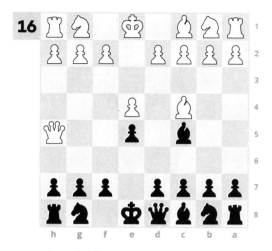

Pick the best move.

A. Knight to f6

B. Pawn to g6

C. Queen to e7

Pick the best move.

A. Queen to f3

B. Queen captures pawn on e5

C. Bishop captures pawn on f7

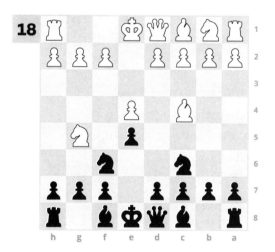

Pick the best move, trying to defend the pawn on f7.

A. Pawn to d5

B. Knight captures pawn on e4

C. Queen to e7

MAKE YOUR PIECES ACTIVE

An active piece is a piece in the middle of the board that can advance far in multiple directions, like the white bishop in diagram 2.4. An inactive piece is a piece that can't move much. For example, the black bishop can only move one square because it's stuck behind pawns.

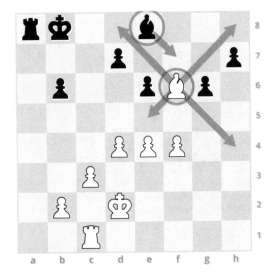

DIAGRAM 2.4: Active vs. inactive bishops

GAIN MATERIAL ADVANTAGE

To have **material advantage** over your opponent means to have more, and a higher value of, pieces on the board. You can gain material advantage by capturing your opponent's pieces without losing too many of your own, especially high-value pieces like the queen, rook, and bishop.

Like having more soldiers on a battlefield, having more pieces can give you more choices and make it tougher for your opponent to defend, giving you a greater chance of winning. If you don't pay attention to material advantage, you might lose chess pieces without gaining anything in return.

Chess is not just about capturing pieces; it's also about protecting your pieces and maintaining strong control of the board. Keep an eye on gaining material advantage, but don't forget about your overall strategy, so you can make smart moves and win the game!

19

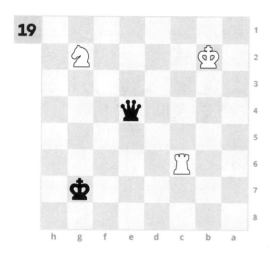

Pick the better capture.

A. Queen to g2

B. Queen to c6

20

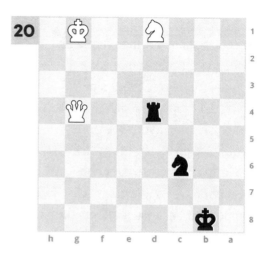

Pick the better capture.

A. Rook to d1

B. Rook to g4

21

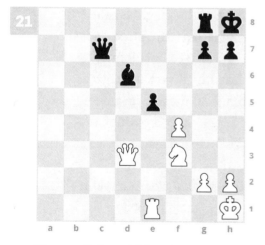

True or False: White should use the pawn on f4 to capture the pawn on e5.

22

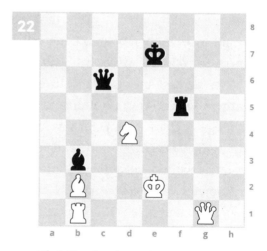

Pick the best capture.

A. Knight to b3

B. Knight to f5

C. Knight to c6

KNOW WHEN TO EXCHANGE (AND WHEN NOT TO)

In chess, an **exchange** happens when you trade one of your pieces for an opponent's piece of equal or near-equal value. For example, if you give up your bishop to capture a bishop or knight, that's an exchange. Knowing when to exchange is important because it affects the balance of power on the chessboard. A great reason to exchange pieces is to gain material advantage. Exchanges can also help you create new threats. When you

DIAGRAM 2.5: A favorable exchange

capture your opponent's piece, they must respond, and that might create weaknesses in their position. In diagram 2.5, white has an extra piece, so it's smart to exchange pieces by using the bishop to capture the knight on d7.

You can exchange in every stage of the game. You might exchange pieces early to develop your position and gain an advantage. In the middle game, strategic exchanges can create weaknesses in your opponent's position or strengthen your own. In the endgame, knowing when to exchange pieces can lead to a winning advantage or draw.

Knowing when *not* to make an exchange is also important. For example, if your opponent's piece is not an active threat, exchanging might not be a good idea, as it could help them improve their position. You also don't want to trade your piece for an opponent's less valuable piece, giving them the advantage.

Consider the value of the pieces, your positions on the board, and your long-term plans before making an exchange. By making smart exchanges, you can outwit your opponent, gain an advantage, and increase your chances of winning!

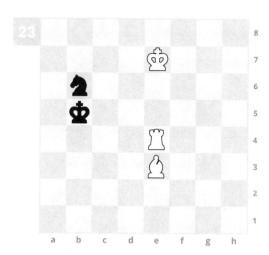

True or False: The best move is bishop captures knight on b6.

Pick the best move.

- A. Rook captures rook on d8
- B. Knight captures bishop on f8
- C. Knight captures rook on d8

Find the good exchange.

Which is the better capture?

- A. Bishop captures bishop on a4
- B. Bishop captures rook on e4

Which is the best exchange?

A. Queen captures pawn on c5

B. Queen captures pawn on b7

C. Queen captures queen on f7

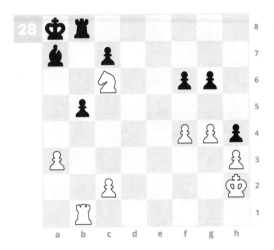

Which is the better exchange?

A. Knight captures bishop on a7

B. Knight captures rook on b8

COUNT YOUR PIECES TO AVOID BLUNDERS

Sometimes, you might make a mistake (known as a blunder in chess) and either move a piece into a dangerous spot or leave it unprotected and at risk, otherwise known as a **hanging piece**.

One way to avoid blunders is to count your pieces. As you're deciding where to move a piece, count how many of your pieces can attack a square and how many of your opponent's pieces can defend it. If you have more attackers than your opponent has defenders, you can capture their piece and win material. Let's say you want to capture your opponent's pawn. Count how many attackers and defenders can move to that square. If you have two attackers (say, a pawn and a bishop) and your opponent only has one defender (a queen), you can capture their pawn and win material.

Before you make any move, take a minute to count your pieces and consider their positions on the board—it's a simple way to avoid blunders.

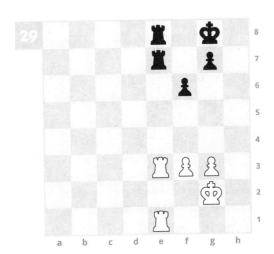

Which black piece is hanging and at risk?

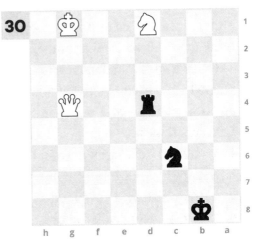

Which white piece is the best hanging piece to capture?

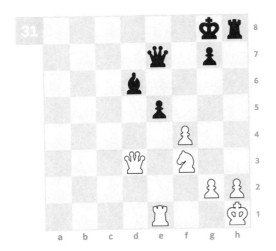

Which black piece is not fully protected?

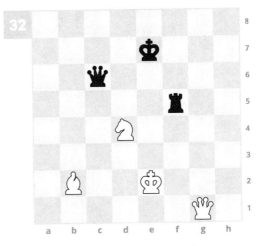

Capture the most powerful hanging black piece.

CHAPTER 3

CENTER, DEVELOP, AND CASTLE

In this chapter, we'll dive deeper into the three opening principles: centering, developing, and making the king safe. These principles will help you start strong and set you up for a good middle game.

CENTER

Centering means to move chess pieces to the middle of the board, especially squares e4, d4, e5, and d5 (see diagram 2.1 on page 25). When we dominate the center, our pieces can move around more easily and we can attack and defend better.

To center your chess pieces:

DIAGRAM 3.1: White has three pawns controlling the center. Black should move to c5 to break white's control.

- Move your two middle pawns two squares forward to the center.
- Move knights and bishops closer to the center. If you're playing as white, move your knights to f3 and c3. If you're playing as black, move your knights to f6 and c6. Move a white bishop to c4 and black bishop to c5.

If you find yourself getting crowded out of the center by your opponent, here are tips to regain control:

- Look for threats. Even if you're pushed back, find ways to create threats in other areas of the board.
- Find weaknesses. Look for weak spots in your opponent's position and try to take advantage of them.
- Move your pawns. Move your pawns forward to challenge your opponent's pieces and create space for your other pieces (see diagram 3.1).
- Defend your king. Keep your king safe. Don't move it forward, and try to keep it defended by pawns, knights, and bishops.

DEVELOP YOUR PIECES

Developing pieces in chess means bringing them out from their starting positions and placing them on active and useful squares. This helps you:

- Control more squares on the board, giving you more opportunities to attack your opponent.
- Use your pieces to support each other and create dominant combinations.
- Protect your king.

This is the ideal order to develop your pieces:

PAWNS: With your first moves, command the center by moving the two center pawns to center positions. This also creates space for your other pieces to come out.

KNIGHTS: Knights can jump over other pieces, making it easier for them to reach the center. Developing your knights early also helps you develop other pieces.

BISHOPS: Bishops are long-range pieces and can be strong when placed on open diagonals. Try to develop your bishops to squares that allow them to control central squares and put pressure on your opponent's pieces.

ROOKS: Connect your rooks by castling (page 42), which helps protect your king and brings your rook closer to the center. Once your rooks are connected, they can work together and control files without pawns, and can be very useful for launching attacks. You can also create batteries, a powerful setup where two rooks work side by side to attack.

QUEEN: Don't develop your queen too early, or you'll be an easy target! Follow the three opening principles: control the center, develop your other pieces, and bring your king to safety first to avoid any early attacks on your queen.

CASTLING

Making your king safe is the third opening principle. We can do this by **castling**—a special double move that allows us to move the king and a rook at the same time. Castling helps:

- Protect the king from potential attacks by building a wall around it.
- Connect the rooks, making them ready to support each other and control important parts of the board—especially the center.

DIAGRAM 3.2: Kingside castling

To castle, there are a few rules to remember:

- Castle early, ideally within the first five to ten moves.
- The king and rook must remain in their original positions before castling.
- All pieces between the king and rook must be developed to allow the king and rook to move freely.
- The king cannot be in check or pass through or land on a square that is being attacked. After all, castling is all about keeping your king defended!

There are two types of castling: kingside and queenside. **Kingside castling** is when the king and the rook castle on the side where your king begins, so right for white and left for black. The king moves two spaces toward the kingside rook, and the rook moves to the opposite side of the king. For example, in diagram 3.2, the white king and rook pass each other as the king moves to g1 and the rook on h1 moves to f1.

Queenside castling (or long-side castling) is when the king and rook castle on the side where your queen begins, so left for white and right for black. The king moves two spaces toward the queenside rook, and the rook moves to the opposite side of the king. Castling queenside takes longer because you need to move more pieces out of the way first. In diagram 3.3, the white king moves to c1 and the rook on a1 moves to d1 (passing each other).

DIAGRAM 3.3: Queenside castling

Castling early is an easy way to set a strong foundation for your game. If your opponent castles before you, don't worry—you don't need to copy them right away! You can focus on developing your other pieces and controlling the center of the board. Also, look for ways to put pressure on your opponent's position or create threats with your pieces. Calmly evaluate the situation, make moves that put you in a good position, and keep your king safe.

Pick the best move.

A. Pawn to g4

B. Pawn to a3

C. Pawn to d4

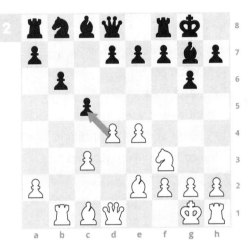

True or False: Capturing the pawn on c5 is a good idea.

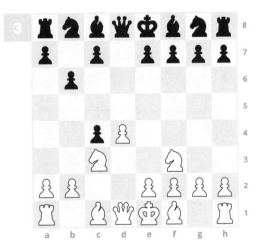

Pick the best move.

A. Pawn to b3

B. Pawn to e4

C. Pawn to h3

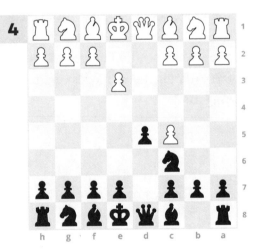

Pick the best move.

A. Pawn to f6

B. Pawn to a6

C. Pawn to e5

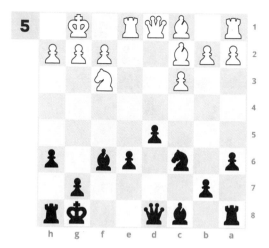

5

Pick the best move.

A. Pawn to b5

B. Pawn to e5

C. Pawn to d4

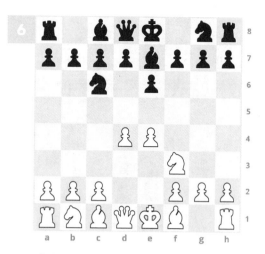

6

Pick the best move.

A. Pawn to c4

B. Bishop to g5

C. Knight to a3

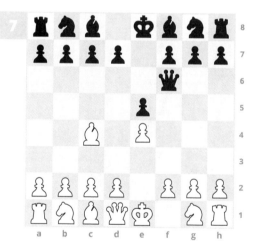

7

Pick the best move.

A. Queen to f3

B. Knight to f3

C. Knight to h3

8

Pick the best move.

A. Knight to c3

B. Knight to g5

C. Bishop to d5

9

Pick the best move.

A. Bishop to c5

B. Bishop to d6

C. Bishop to b4

10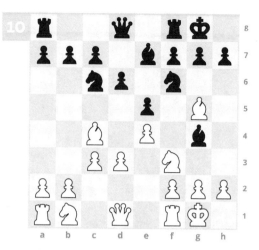

Pick the best move.

A. King to h1

B. Bishop to h4

C. Knight on b1 to d2

11

Pick the best move.

A. Pawn to b6

B. Bishop to b4

C. Knight to a6

12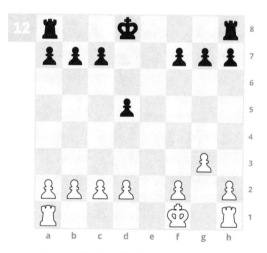

True or False: White cannot castle anymore.

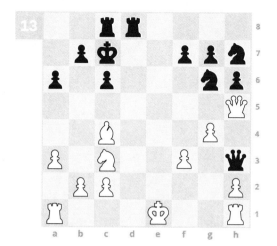

True or False: White can castle.

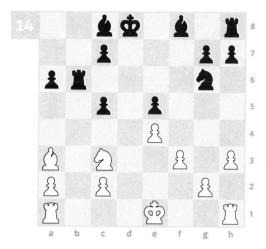

True or False: White can castle kingside and queenside.

True or False: White can't castle kingside.

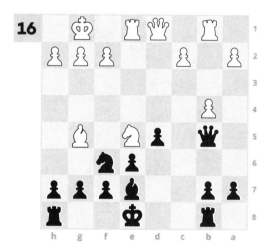

To castle kingside, move _____.

CHAPTER 4

CHECK (AND GETTING OUT OF IT!)

One of the most important things to learn in chess is how to put your opponent in check, moving you closer to winning the game. In this chapter you'll learn how, along with how to defend your king and practice escaping from check.

Once you've developed your pieces and have good control over the center, start exploring the board for opportunities. Look for weaknesses such as hanging pieces or a poorly defended king.

As you do this, don't forget to consider your own safety and the overall position of the game. Sometimes it's better to develop your pieces further or create threats before going for a check. Always remember your king's safety and try to anticipate possible countermoves.

Three common tactics for putting your opponent in check are discovered check, double check, and cross-check.

DISCOVERED CHECK

A **discovered check** occurs when you move a piece to reveal a direct attack by another one of your pieces, putting your opponent's king in check. Look to see which of your pieces might be blocking a check opportunity. Just make sure your discovered check doesn't leave your king defenseless!

In diagram 4.1, white has set up a discovered check opportunity by moving its queen to e6. White can now move its knight to d8, which allows its queen to put

DIAGRAM 4.1: Discovered check

the black king in check and block the black rook on b8 from controlling the back rank. The black king will have to move to either f8 or h8, but either way, white can deliver a checkmate on e8.

Double Check

Double check is like a super-powered version of a discovered check. Not only does the unseen piece check the enemy king, but the piece that moved also joins in! The king can't capture or block either of the checking pieces, so it must move away.

In diagram 4.2, white sets up a double check by moving its queen to c6 and capturing the knight, putting the king in check. To escape, the black king must capture the white queen, but now it is hanging in the center of the board. White's running out of attackers, but they're perfectly positioned!

In diagram 4.3, you'll see what happens next. White moves its knight to e5 and now controls d7, the bishop on e3 controls c5, the pawn on a4 controls b5, and the bishop on g2 controls the h1–a8 diagonal. With nowhere to move, the black king is in checkmate.

DIAGRAM 4.2: Double check, part 1

DIAGRAM 4.3: Double check, part 2

CROSS-CHECK

A **cross-check** is when a check is played in response to being put in check. Here, you put your opponent's king in check *and* attack the piece that was putting you in check.

In diagram 4.4, the white king is in check from the black queen. If they traded queens, it would be a draw. (If we only have a knight or a bishop left on the board with two kings, it is impossible to checkmate. It is only possible to checkmate with at least a bishop and a knight, or two bishops.) If the white king moves to g2, the black queen can capture the white queen on b6, but then the white knight would just capture the black queen—the game still ends in a draw. Instead, white should move its knight to c7, because that will block the check to its king *and* check the black king, which has no escape. Black's queen could capture the knight on c7, but then it will be captured by white's queen.

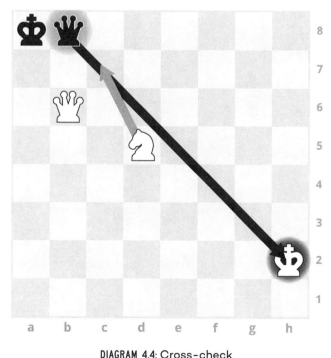

DIAGRAM 4.4: Cross-check

YOUR TURN!

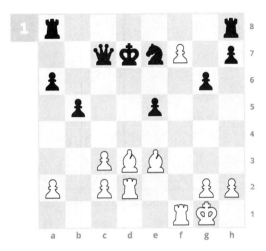

Find two double checks.

A. Bishop to f5 and bishop captures pawn on b5

B. Bishop captures pawn on b5 and bishop to e4

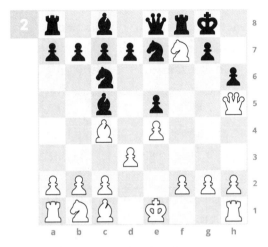

Deliver a double check.

A. Knight to d6

B. Knight captures pawn on h6

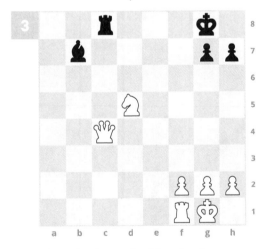

Pick the best double check.

A. Knight to f6

B. Knight to e7

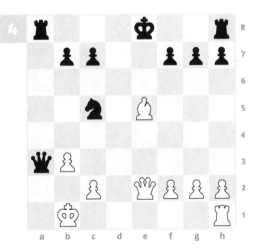

Pick the best discovered check.

A. Bishop captures pawn on g7

B. Bishop to b2

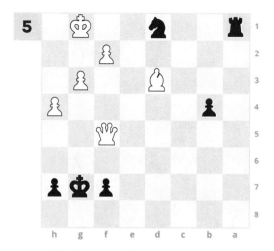

5

Pick the best discovered check.

A. Knight captures pawn on f2

B. Knight to b2

C. Knight to e3

6

Pick the best move.

A. Knight to d6

B. Knight to f6

C. Knight to c5

7

Pick the best move.

A. Bishop to c5

B. Bishop captures pawn on g7

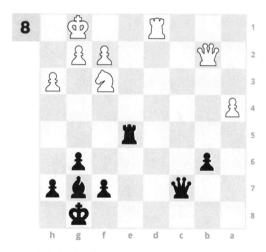

8

Pick the best move.

A. Rook to e2

B. Rook to b5

C. Rook to e1

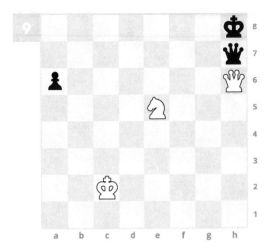

9 Your king is in check. Make a cross-check move.

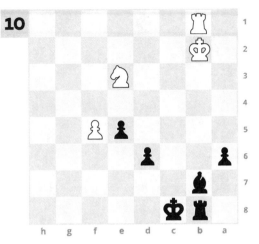

10 Find the best discovered check.

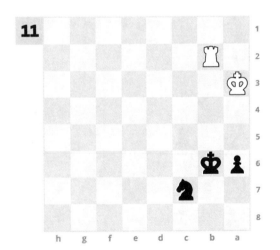

11 Find a cross-check.

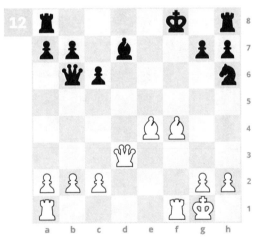

12 True or False: Bishop to e3 is a cross-check.

ESCAPING CHECK

Even if you're in check, there are ways to turn the game around. In diagram 4.5, the king on a5 is in check from the rook on g5. Let's use this example to try three common tactics for escaping check, known as **CPR**: capture, protect, and run away.

CAPTURE: Sometimes you can escape check by capturing the piece that has your king in check. In diagram 4.6, the bishop on e7 could capture the rook on g5 and stop the check. But first ask yourself: If I leave my king where it is and use a different piece (white bishop) to capture the piece attacking my king (black rook), will my king be safe from other pieces?

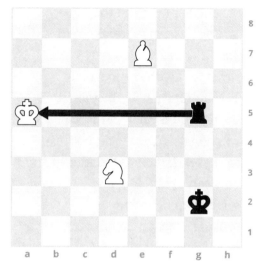

DIAGRAM 4.5: King in check

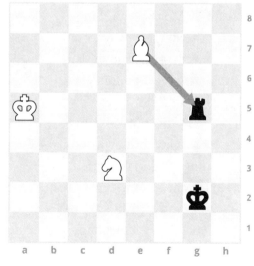

DIAGRAM 4.6: Capture

PROTECT: Protecting, or blocking, is where you move a piece in between your king and the attacking piece. Be careful not to move a piece to block if that leaves it (or another important piece) unprotected. In diagram 4.7, white could block the check by moving its knight to e5, but then the black rook would immediately capture it. Knight to c5 would be a better move because the bishop can protect it. (The best move here for white is to use the bishop to capture the rook.)

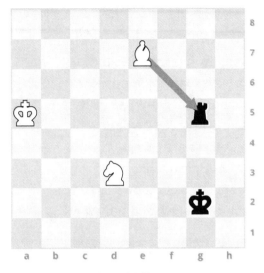

DIAGRAM 4.7: Protect

RUN AWAY: Moving your king away is the simplest way to escape check. Avoid moving it to a square where it might get trapped or attacked again. In diagram 4.8, the king can run away by moving to a6, b6, or b4.

Escaping checks is an essential skill in chess. Sometimes you might even combine two or more tactics. Look at diagram 4.8 again. You could have your

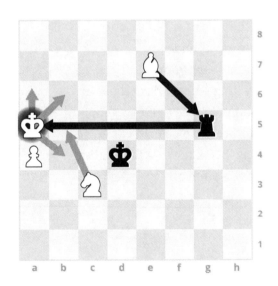

DIAGRAM 4.8: Run away

king run away to b4, a6, or b6 *and* use your bishop to capture the black rook on g5, which would eliminate the attacker. Or you can play a cross-check by moving your knight to b5, which would block their check *and* check their king.

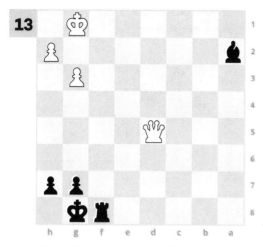

13

Pick the best escape from check.

A. King to h8

B. Bishop captures queen on d5

14

Pick the best escape from check.

A. King to h7

B. Knight captures rook on d8

15

Find the best escape from check.

16

Pick the better escape from check.

A. Queen to d7

B. Bishop to d7

17

Pick the best escape from check.

- A. Knight to e3
- B. Knight to d4
- C. Rook to f2

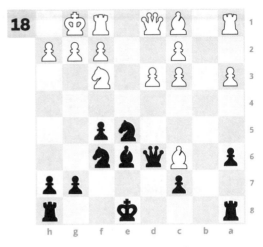

18

Pick the better escape from check.

- A. King to e7
- B. Knight captures bishop on c6

19

True or False: The black king is in check.

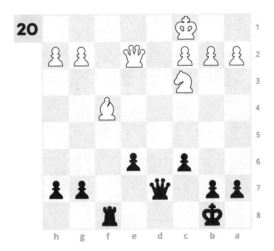

20

Find the best escape from check.

21

Pick the best escape from check.

A. King to e4

B. Rook to d3

C. King to f2

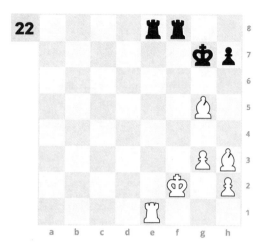

22

Pick the best escape from check.

A. King to g1

B. Bishop to f5

C. Bishop to f4

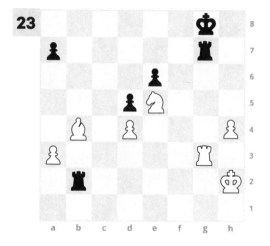

23

Pick the best escape from check.

A. Rook to g2

B. Bishop to d2

C. King to h3

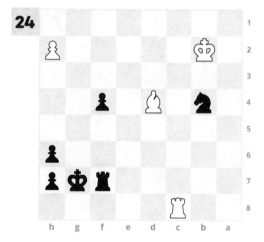

24

True or False: The king on b2 is in check.

CHAPTER 5

ALL ABOUT PAWNS

In this chapter, we'll dive into the fascinating world of pawns. These little warriors might seem simple, but they hold incredible power on the chessboard.

PAWN TYPES

There are several types of pawns in chess. Each type of pawn has its own strengths and weaknesses, and understanding them can help you make better strategic decisions. We learned about regular pawns in chapter 1, but here are some others:

ISOLATED PAWNS: An **isolated pawn** is a pawn that doesn't have any other pawns of the same color on neighboring files. This can make it difficult to defend, especially in the endgame.

PASSED PAWNS: A **passed pawn** is one whose file is not blocked by an opponent's pawn and who can advance freely. This makes it very powerful because it can be promoted to a queen, rook, bishop, or knight if it reaches the other side of the board (more on this soon!).

BACKWARD PAWNS: A **backward pawn** is a pawn that's behind its neighboring pawn(s) and can't be protected by them. It can be very difficult to defend backward pawns, so advance it forward when possible.

DIAGRAM 5.1: Isolated pawn on d4

DIAGRAM 5.2: Passed pawn on a4

DIAGRAM 5.3: Backward pawn on c3

DOUBLED PAWNS: Doubled pawns are two pawns of the same color on the same file. This can make it difficult to protect them both and limits their mobility. Doubled pawns should be avoided except in the opening, when they're defending central squares such as e6 (controlling f5 and d5) and e5 (controlling f4 and d4).

DIAGRAM 5.4: Doubled pawns on f5 and f6

PAWN STRUCTURES

Pawns become much more powerful when they work together! In this section, we'll explore some ways that pawns can join forces to defend and attack.

CONNECTED PAWNS

Connected pawns are two or more pawns of the same color positioned closely on adjacent files. They can make it difficult for the opponent to attack them. Connected pawns work together, advancing as a group, putting pressure on their opponent, and protecting each other along the way.

DIAGRAM 5.5: Connected pawns on b6 and c5

PAWN SHIELDS

After castling, it's important to create a **pawn shield**, or a row of pawns in front of your king, to defend it. Pawn shields prevent your opponent's pieces from moving easily

DIAGRAM 5.6: Pawn shield

through those squares and buy you time to develop your other pieces and plan next moves.

To build a pawn shield:

- Choose three pawns that are next to each other in the same row (see diagram 5.6).
- Move those pawns forward as needed (h3 is a typical first move and creates space for the king to move in the future).
- Keep your pawns together, in a row, in front of your king.

Pawn Chains

A **pawn chain** is a diagonal chain of pawns that work together, protecting each other from attack.

Pawn chains also:

- Protect your pieces (especially your king) from threats.
- Help you control more squares on the board, giving you a space advantage (see page 110).
- Open paths for your other pieces to attack.

DIAGRAM 5.7: Pawn chain

To create an effective pawn chain, start with three pawns of the same color in a row, side by side. Move one of the pawns on the end up two squares with its first move, then move the middle pawn up one. The pawn on the other end is the bottom end of the diagonal. Move these pawns together, so the chain remains connected.

SPECIAL RULES FOR PAWNS

Let's talk about two special rules just for pawns: en passant and pawn promotion.

EN PASSANT

If an opposing pawn moves two squares on its first move and lands next to your pawn, you may capture that pawn **en passant** (which means "in passing") on your next move, as if it had only moved one square. The en passant capture must be made immediately; otherwise, the opportunity is lost.

DIAGRAM 5.8: En passant

In diagram 5.8, the white pawn moves from b2 to b4, so it's next to the black pawn on a4. The black pawn can capture it en passant. To do so, the black pawn moves diagonally to b3—the square where the white pawn would have been if it had only moved forward one square. Then black can remove the white pawn on b4.

PAWN PROMOTION

Pawn promotion allows a pawn to become any other piece—except for a king—when it reaches the opposite end of the board. Players usually promote their pawns to queens because it's the most powerful piece. And you can have more than one promoted queen—in fact, up to eight, since there are eight pawns! (In case you're curious, pieces from other chess sets are used to fill in as the promoted piece.)

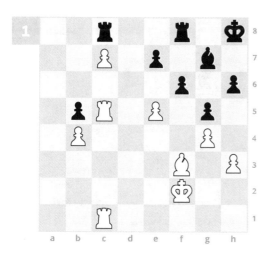

True or False: The pawn on c7 is a backward pawn.

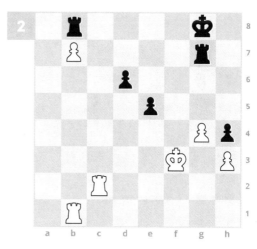

Identify white's two passed pawns.

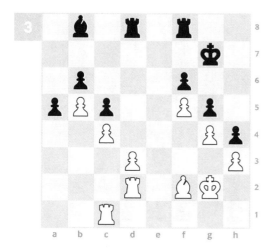

True or False: The pawn on d3 is a backward pawn.

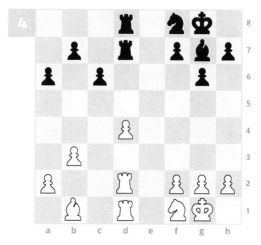

Identify the isolated pawn.

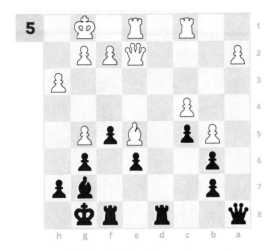

5

Which is the backward pawn?

A. h7

B. e6

C. f5

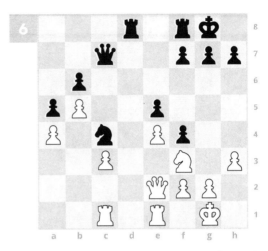

6

True or False: The pawns on f2 and g2 are doubled pawns.

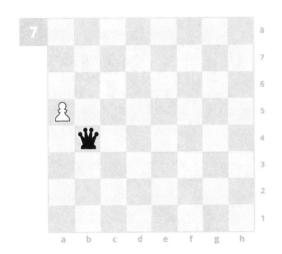

7

How many moves will it take to promote the pawn?

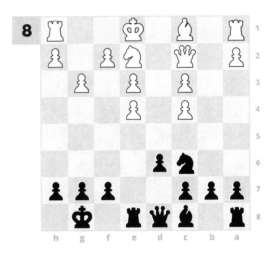

8

True or False: Black has a better pawn structure protecting the king.

True or False: The pawn on f3 is preventing checkmate.

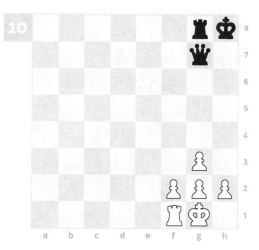

True or False: The pawn on g3 is preventing checkmate.

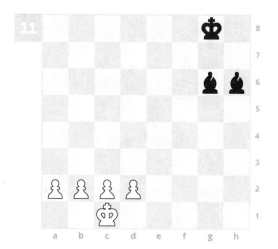

True or False: The pawns on a2, b2, c2, and d2 are a pawn chain.

True or False: The pawns on a4, b4, and c4 are called connected pawns.

13

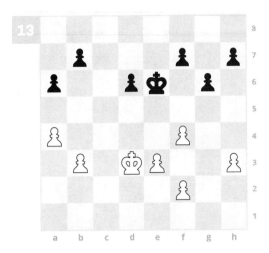

True or False: The pawns on e3 and h3 are called doubled pawns.

14

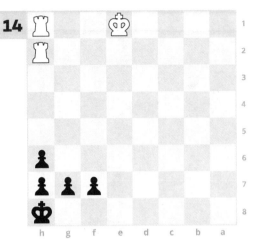

Which pawn is preventing the rook on h2 from capturing the pawn on h7?

15

True or False: The pawn on b5 is an isolated pawn.

16

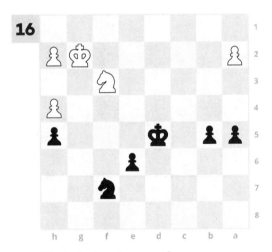

Find the best move for a pawn.

A. Pawn to e5

B. Pawn to a4

C. Pawn to b4

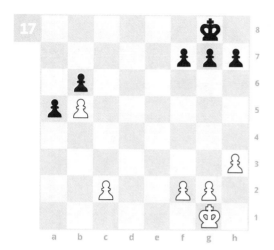

Black just moved a pawn from a7 to a5. What's your best move?

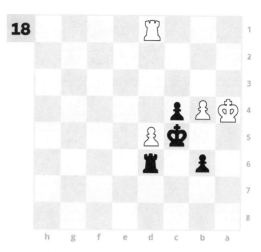

White just moved a pawn from b2 to b4. Stop it from checking your king.

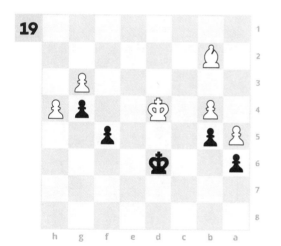

White just moved a pawn from h2 to h4. What's your best move?

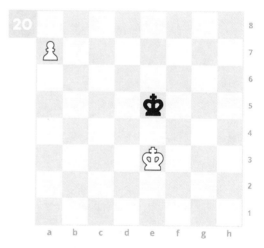

True or False: When the white pawn moves to a8, it can be promoted to any piece.

True or False: If the white pawn moves to a8, it can be promoted to a queen or rook and deliver a checkmate.

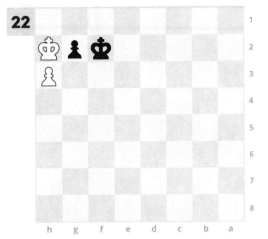

If the pawn on g2 moves to g1, to deliver a checkmate in one move, it should be promoted to:

    A. Rook

    B. Bishop

    C. Queen

CHAPTER 6

ATTACK, ATTACK, ATTACK

Let's go on the attack! In this chapter, we'll cover some broad attacking ideas and then practice specific attacking moves. Learning how to launch an effective and coordinated attack will improve your chances of gaining material and winning the game.

ATTACKING IDEAS

Before we jump into specific attacking moves, let's explore some ideas. There are three common ways to launch a direct attack in chess.

ATTACKING TWO PIECES: Also known as a **double attack** (see page 73), you target two of the enemy's pieces at the same time. This forces your opponent to choose which piece to defend, giving you the opportunity to capture the other one. Knights and queens are most effective at this, but as diagram 6.1 shows, even a pawn can attack two pieces.

ATTACKING FROM THE BACK: Here you'll start an attack on your opponent's pieces from behind (or the side). You can catch your opponent unprepared and disrupt their plans, giving you the opportunity to gain an advantage. Again, knights and queens are particularly effective at this, due to their unique movement abilities.

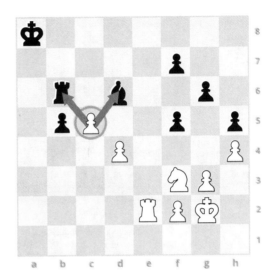

DIAGRAM 6.1: The pawn is targeting the rook and bishop

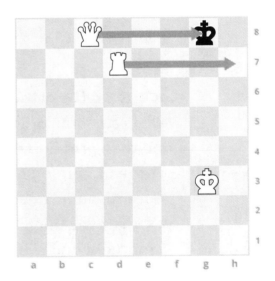

DIAGRAM 6.2: A queen-and-rook checkmate, where the queen and rook work together to threaten the opposition's king, is an example of an attack from behind.

ATTACKING A LINE: This strategy involves positioning long-range pieces (the queen, rooks, and bishops) to attack multiple squares in a straight line. By controlling important lines on the board, you can dominate entire areas, put pressure on several pieces, and limit their options.

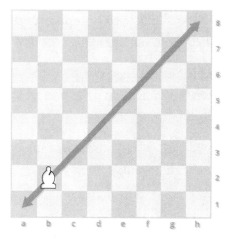

DIAGRAM 6.3: The bishop is free to attack all along the diagonal

TYPES OF DOUBLE ATTACKS

Sometimes the purpose of a double attack is to win material. Other times, the goal is to checkmate and win outright! There are two kinds of double attacks: forks and discovered attacks.

FORK

A **fork** is when a single piece attacks two or more pieces. A classic example is the knight fork. In diagram 6.4, when the knight moves to e5, it can simultaneously threaten the black queen and king—that's pretty powerful!

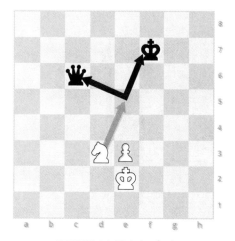

DIAGRAM 6.4: Knight fork

QUEEN FORK: Because of the queen's long-range powers and its ability to move in any direction, it's easy for it to fork two pieces on opposite ends of the board.

BISHOP FORK: Look for opportunities where your bishop can slide between two of your opponent's pieces and attack them both.

PAWN FORK: When two pieces are standing side by side with one square between them, that's the perfect spot for your pawn to slide in (see diagram 6.1 on page 72).

ROOK FORK: Rooks are long-range powerhouses. They can attack pieces far across their rank or file.

DISCOVERED ATTACKS

Much like a discovered check (page 49), a **discovered attack** is a surprise attack where you move one of your pieces to uncover a hidden attacking piece behind it. A discovered attack can threaten to win material (diagram 6.5) or even checkmate the enemy king (diagram 6.6).

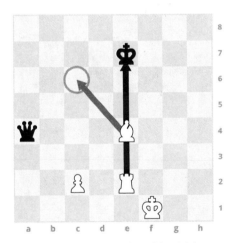

DIAGRAM 6.5: Moving the white bishop to c6 creates an attack on the queen (by the bishop) and uncovers an attack on the king (by the rook). Black must move its king, so the bishop can capture the queen.

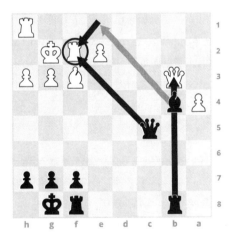

DIAGRAM 6.6: Moving the black bishop to e1 both uncovers an attack on the queen (by the rook) and further threatens the rook (with the bishop and the black queen). The white queen will run away, leaving the black queen to capture the rook on f2 and deliver a checkmate.

1

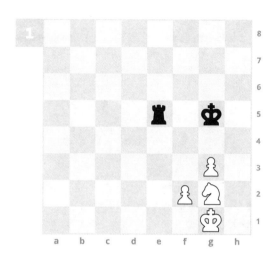

Which move forks two pieces?

2

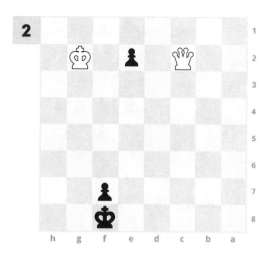

Which move forks two pieces?

3

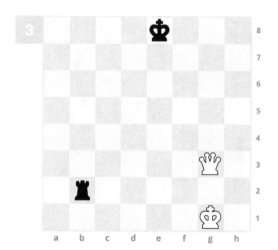

Which move forks two pieces without exposing the queen to an attack?

4

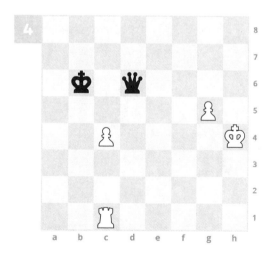

Which move forks two pieces?

ATTACK, ATTACK, ATTACK 75

5

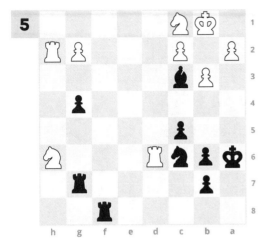

Find the best move to fork two pieces.

6

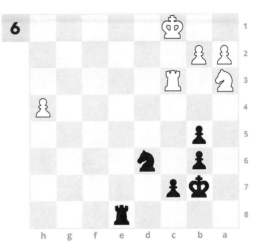

Find the best move to fork two pieces.

7

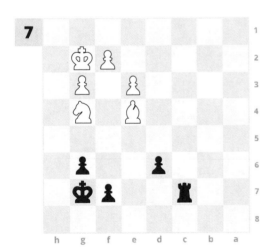

Which move forks two pieces?

A. Rook to c4

B. Pawn to d5

C. Pawn to f5

8

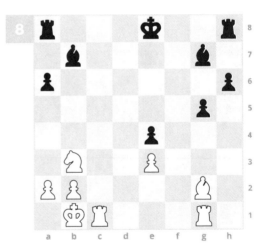

Which move forks two pieces?

A. Knight to c5

B. Rook to c7

C. Knight to a5

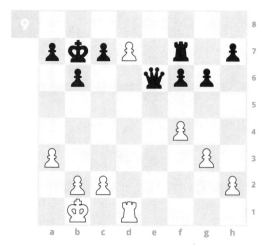

Find a move to fork two valuable pieces.

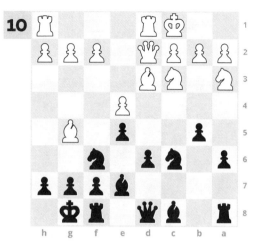

Which move forks two pieces?

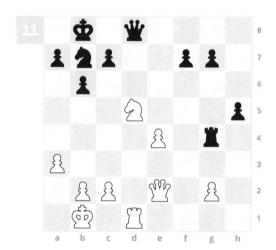

Set up to win a piece using a discovered attack.

A. Knight to b4

B. Knight to e3

C. Knight to c7

Set up to win a piece using a discovered attack.

A. Pawn to e5

B. Bishop to b2

C. Knight captures pawn on d6

13

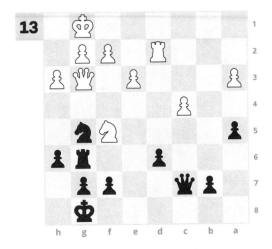

Set up to win a piece using a discovered attack.

A. Knight to f3

B. Knight captures pawn on h3

C. Knight to e4

14

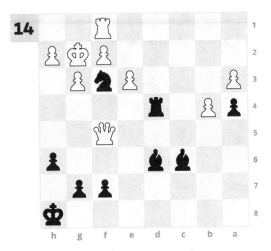

Set up to win a piece using a discovered attack.

A. Knight to d2

B. Knight to h4

C. Knight captures pawn on h2

15

Set up to win a piece using a discovered attack that results in check.

16

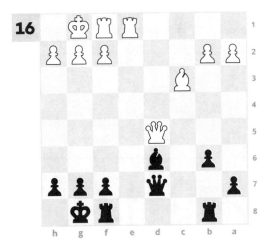

Set up to win a piece using a discovered attack that results in check.

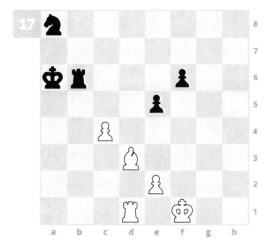

17

Set up to win a piece using a discovered attack that results in check.

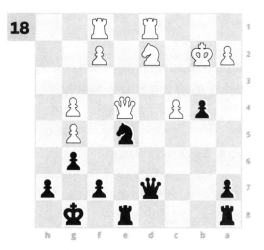

18

Set up to win a piece using a discovered attack that results in check.

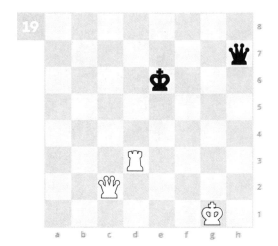

19

Set up to win a piece using a discovered attack that results in check.

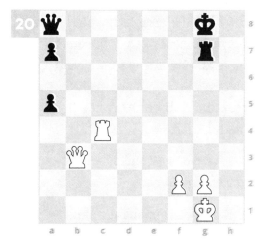

20

Set up to win a piece using a discovered attack that results in check.

PINS

A **pin** is a tactic in which one of your pieces traps an opponent's piece, making it unable to move to defend other pieces or squares. Pins create opportunities for you to attack or gain control. There are two types of pins: absolute and relative.

ABSOLUTE PIN: An **absolute pin** freezes an opponent's piece in place, making it unable to move without putting their own king in danger (see diagram 6.7). The queen, rook, and bishop are the most powerful pinners.

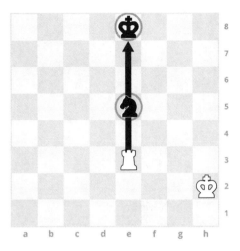

DIAGRAM 6.7: The white rook has the black knight in an absolute pin

RELATIVE PIN: A **relative pin** limits the movement of an opponent's piece and threatens a more valuable piece of theirs, but not the king. The rook and bishop are great at pulling off this trick.

After you've pinned a piece, you can:

DIAGRAM 6.8: The white bishop has the black knight in a relative pin

- Keep your opponent's pinned piece trapped and limit their movement.
- Focus your attention on attacking other pieces or your opponent's king.
- Plan next moves and use the pinned piece as a target for future attacks.

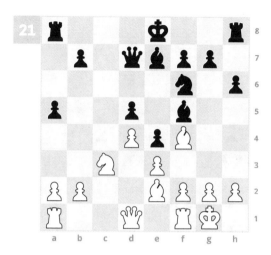

Which is an absolute pin?

A. Bishop to e5

B. Bishop to b5

C. Bishop to g4

Which is an absolute pin?

A. Bishop to c4

B. Rook to d1

C. Bishop to f3

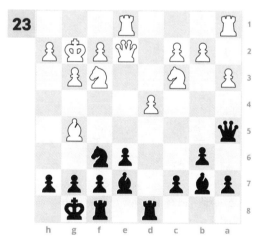

Identify the pinned piece and capture the piece it is defending.

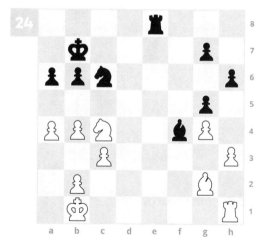

Attack the pinned piece in two moves.

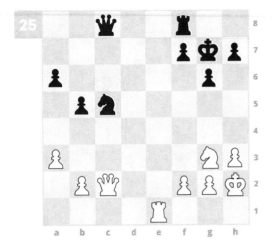

Put more pressure on the pinned piece.

A. Knight to e4

B. Queen to c3

C. Rook to c1

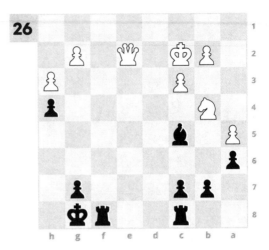

Find the absolute pin.

A. Rook to f2

B. Rook to e8

C. Bishop captures knight on b4

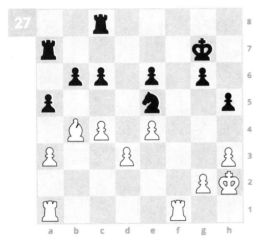

Find the absolute pin.

A. Bishop to c3

B. Bishop to d6

C. Bishop to d2

Find checkmate in one move using an absolute pin.

A. Bishop captures pawn on g6

B. Rook to h8

C. Queen captures knight on h5

SKEWERS

A **skewer** is like a magic trick that can make your opponent's piece move, revealing another piece behind it. Queens, rooks, and bishops are particularly good at this trick.

ABSOLUTE SKEWER: An **absolute skewer** occurs when the piece being directly attacked is the king. The king *must* move to get out of check, and in doing so, reveals another piece that can be captured (see diagram 6.9).

RELATIVE SKEWER: A **relative skewer** makes a more valuable piece (but not the king) move, revealing a less valuable piece hiding behind it.

After completing a skewer, you can:

- Capture the less important piece that was revealed.
- Put more pressure on the valuable piece that moved.

DIAGRAM 6.9: White moved its rook so it could check black's king. The king must move, revealing the rook behind it.

DIAGRAM 6.10: The white bishop has skewered the black queen. She's likely to move and reveal the rook behind her.

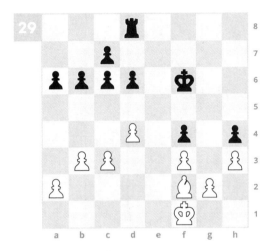

Create a skewer.

A. Pawn to d5

B. Bishop captures pawn on h4

C. Bishop to e1

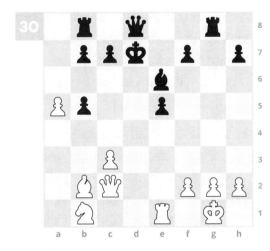

Create a skewer.

A. Rook to d1

B. Queen captures pawn on h7

C. Queen to e4

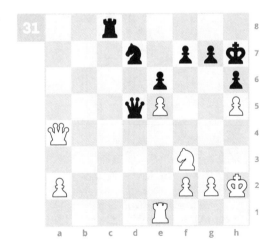

Create a skewer.

A. Queen to a6

B. Rook to d1

C. Queen to e4

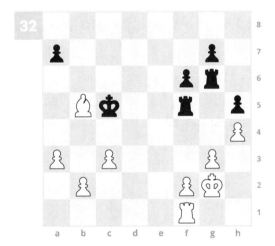

Find the best skewer.

A. Bishop to e8

B. Bishop to d7

C. Bishop to d3

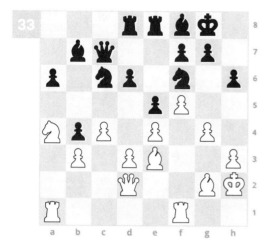

Create a skewer.

- A. Bishop to b6
- B. Bishop to g5
- C. Pawn to c5

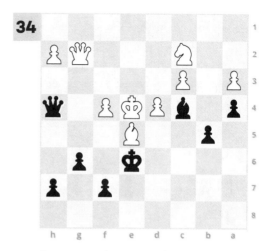

Create a skewer.

- A. Pawn to f5
- B. Bishop to d3
- C. Bishop to d5

Create a skewer.

- A. Bishop to d6
- B. Bishop to h6
- C. Queen to b2

Create a skewer.

- A. Pawn to d5
- B. Bishop to h3
- C. Bishop to c4

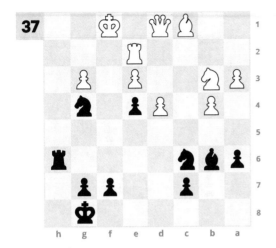

37

Create a skewer.

A. Rook to f6

B. Knight captures pawn on e3

C. Rook to h1

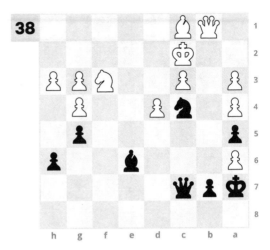

38

Create a skewer.

A. Bishop to f5

B. Knight captures pawn on a3

C. Queen to h7

CHAPTER 7

DESTROY THEIR DEFENSE

Let's talk defense! We will explore how to capture or lure away a defender. You'll also learn what actions to take once you successfully lure a defender away.

CAPTURING A DEFENDER

When you capture an opponent's defender, you're removing a piece that was protecting their other pieces or squares. This can weaken your opponent's position, give you a material advantage, and potentially help you win the game.

Consider:

- Can your piece capture the defender without being captured?
- Will the move put any of your other pieces in danger?
- Is it a trap? Your opponent might be planting a decoy, sacrificing their less valuable piece to attack or capture your more valuable piece.

There are two main strategies:

CAPTURE THE DEFENDER: You capture the piece that's defending an important piece or square (see diagram 7.1).

OVERLOAD THE DEFENDER: Instead of directly capturing the defender, you pressure it with multiple pieces. This forces the defender to choose which piece to protect, leaving the others unprotected.

DIAGRAM 7.1: The knight on d5 is defending the rook on f4. The white bishop captures the knight, so the white rook can capture the rook on f4.

DIAGRAM 7.2: Overloading the black pawn defender

In diagram 7.2, the black pawn on b5 is defending the bishop on c4 and the knight on a4, both of which are under pressure. The white knight can capture the bishop on c4, which leads the black pawn to capture it. That leaves the black knight on a4 unprotected.

1

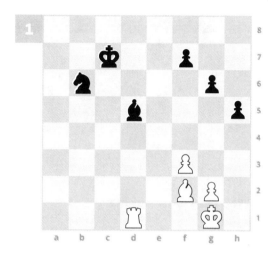

Find the best way to remove a defender.

2

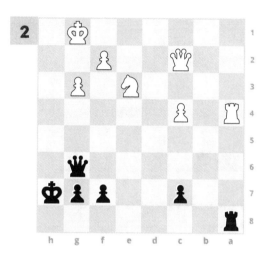

Find the best way to remove a defender.

3

Find the best way to remove a defender.

4

Find the best way to remove a defender.

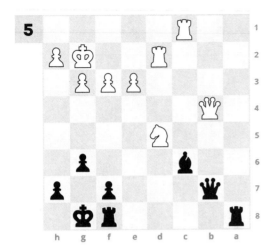

5

Find the best way to remove a defender.

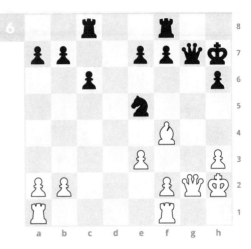

6

Find the best way to remove a defender.

7

Find the best way to remove a defender.

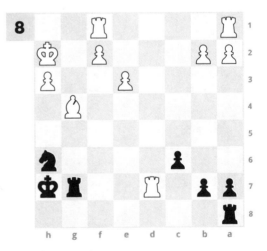

8

Find the best way to remove a defender.

9

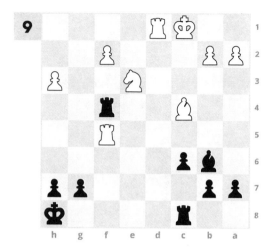

Find the best move to remove a defender that results in check.

10

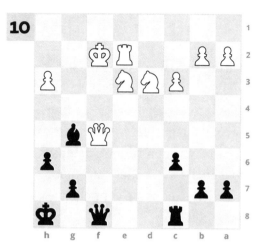

Find the best move to remove a defender that results in check.

11

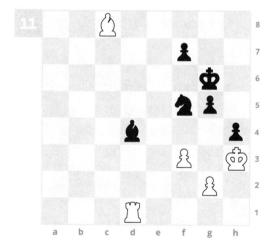

Find the best move to remove a defender that results in check.

LURING AWAY A DEFENDER

Luring away a defender means tricking an opponent into moving their piece away from defending a more valuable piece. This tactic can weaken the opposition's defense and create more attacking opportunities, expanding your chance of winning!

DIAGRAM 7.3: Luring away the black knight defender

Just like in soccer, you can lure away a defender by pretending to go in one direction and then quickly changing direction. For example, you might make a move that looks like you're going to attack one side of the board, and the opponent's defender might move there to protect it. While they're focused on that side, you can quickly switch your attack to the other side, where their defenses are weaker.

In diagram 7.3, white is luring the black knight defender away by moving its pawn to c6, so the knight will move to avoid being captured (by jumping away to f6, for example). Then the rook on e1 can capture the bishop on e5. Even after that white pawn moves, if black moves its bishop to c3, the white rook can still move to c1 to continue attacking the bishop. Or if after that white pawn moves, black moves its bishop to f6, the white pawn will just capture the knight on d7.

Before you execute a lure, keep these important points in mind:

- **Check for weak areas.** Always look at both sides of the board for weaknesses. A common mistake is to focus on one side of the board and overlook potential threats on the other side.
- **Choose the right moment.** Look for chances when the opponent's defenders are distracted or focused on a different area.
- **Make sure your own pieces are safe.** Avoid making moves that leave your pieces vulnerable.
- **Consider the consequences.** Predict how the opponent might respond to your lure. Calculate the risks and benefits of each move you make.
- **Consider the value of each piece involved.** If you can capture a more valuable piece by luring away a defender, it's worth it.
- **Be cautious of traps.** Your opponent might sacrifice a less valuable piece to pull you into capturing it, only to set up a trap and gain an advantage. Be on the lookout for hidden motives.
- **Think big-picture.** Consider how the board will change after the lure and whether it fits with your long-term goals.

Find the best move to lure away the defender.

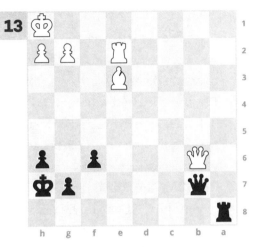

Lure away the defender.

Find the best move to lure away the defender.

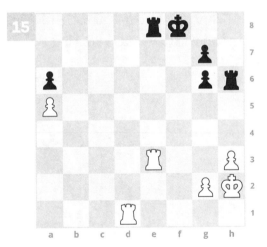

Lure away the defender.

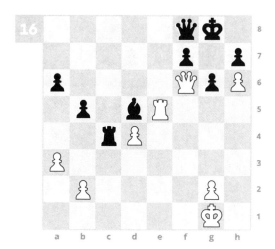

Lure away the defender.

Find the best move to lure away the defender.

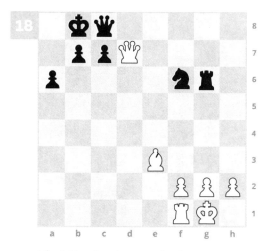

Find the best move to lure away the defender.

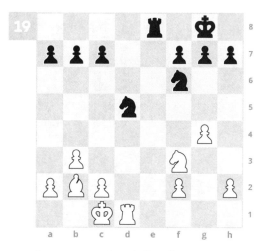

Lure away the defender.

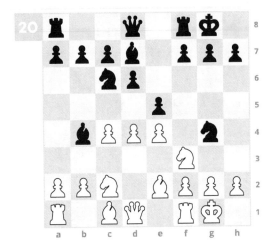

20

Lure away the defender.

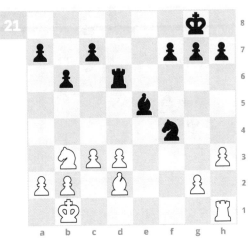

21

Lure away the defender.

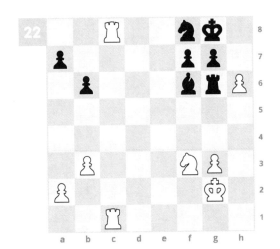

22

Find the best move to lure away the defender.

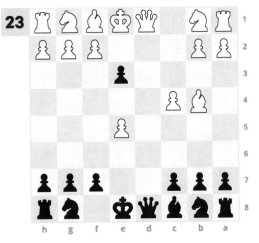

23

Find the best move to lure away the defender.

CHAPTER 8

CHECKMATES IN THE MIDDLE GAME

During the middle game, many players become super focused on attacking or defending individual pieces, but keep an eye out for checkmate opportunities! In this chapter, we'll dive into middle game checkmate patterns and learn about situations where neither player can achieve checkmate, resulting in a draw.

COMMON MIDDLE GAME CHECKMATES

The following checkmate patterns are great choices in the middle game because they use two or more pieces working together, and you tend to have more pieces to use during the middle game than in the endgame.

BACK-RANK CHECKMATE: Imagine a castle with tall walls at the back. The back-rank checkmate happens when the opponent's king gets trapped behind those walls and can't run away. To create a back-rank checkmate, you need to coordinate your pieces, especially rooks or the queen. They can attack the back rank, where the king is hiding, cornering the king and making sure it has no safe squares to run to. Be careful not to leave your own back rank vulnerable—keep at least one rook or the queen next to the king.

DIAGRAM 8.1: Back-rank checkmate. The black rook is checkmating the white king; the king has no escape. (Black's back rank is also vulnerable!)

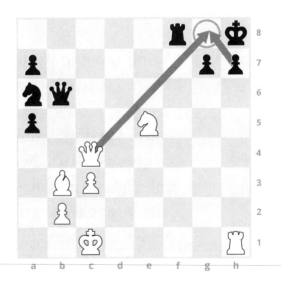

DIAGRAM 8.2: Smothered checkmate

SMOTHERED CHECKMATE: This occurs when the opponent's king is surrounded by its own pieces and has no place to go. In diagram 8.2, the black king is surrounded by its rook and pawns. In this case, you would sacrifice your white queen by moving it to g8 and letting it be captured by the black rook to block the king's escape squares, and then let your knight deliver the checkmate by moving to f7.

DIAGRAM 8.3: White can checkmate the king by using the queen to capture the black pawn and check the king as the white pawn protects the queen.

ASSISTED CHECKMATE: This is when one piece assists another piece to deliver checkmate (see diagram 8.3). The assisting piece controls important squares, preventing the king's escape, while the other piece delivers the final blow.

LAWNMOWER CHECKMATE: Imagine a lawnmower moving back and forth, cutting grass in a straight line. This checkmate works similarly. You move your rook or queen horizontally or vertically, cutting off the opponent's king's escape squares one by one until the king gets stuck. Make sure to protect your lawnmower piece and prevent any counterplay from your opponent.

DIAGRAM 8.4: Lawnmower checkmate. The black king is in checkmate from the rook on h2.

PUSHING/TRAPPING PATTERN:

The pushing/trapping pattern is when you trap the opponent's king by pushing it to the corner or a small area of the board. You'll use your pieces to create a net around the king, giving it fewer and fewer options to move.

DIAGRAM 8.5: The king on h8 is trapped and checkmated by the rook on g8. It can't move to h7 (checkmated by the knight) or g7 (still checkmated by the rook).

DRAWS

A draw is when a game ends without a winner. Draws can teach important lessons about strategy and planning. They can happen in these ways:

STALEMATE: This occurs when it's a player's turn to move, their king is not in check, and they don't have any legal moves available. This can happen when a player's pieces accidentally block their own king, or when their pieces prevent any legal moves. Try to avoid getting into stalemate by making sure your king always has a square to move to.

THREEFOLD REPETITION: If players repeat the same moves and positions on the board three times in a row, the game is a draw. This rule stops players from repeating moves over and over (see diagram 8.6).

FIFTY-MOVE RULE: If no pawns are moved and no pieces are captured by either player in the last fifty moves, the game ends in a draw. This rule makes sure the game keeps moving forward.

INSUFFICIENT MATERIAL: If both players have only their kings left on the board, or if one player has only their king and a bishop or knight, it's not possible to checkmate the opponent, so the game ends in a draw.

PERPETUAL CHECK: When a player checks the opponent's king in the same place three times, it is considered a draw.

DRAW BY AGREEMENT: This draw happens when players reach a position in which neither side can win, or when certain rules are met.

DIAGRAM 8.6: Black's last move was queen to a5 (check), then white moved its bishop to d2 (check). Repeating these movements three times would result in a draw. White can avoid this by playing pawn to c3 instead.

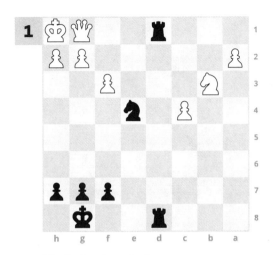

Find checkmate in one move.

A. Knight to g3

B. Rook captures queen on g1

C. Knight to f2

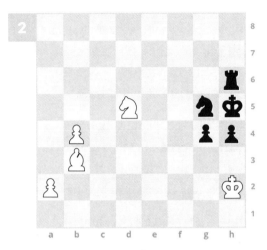

Find checkmate in one move.

A. Knight to f6

B. Knight to f4

C. Bishop to d1

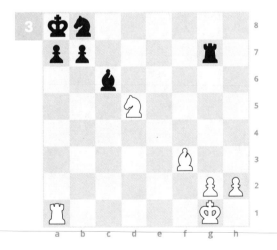

Find checkmate in one move.

A. Knight to c7

B. Rook captures pawn on a7

C. Knight to b6

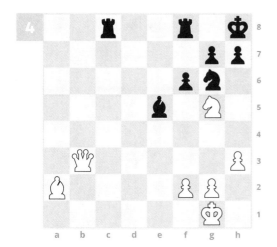

Find checkmate in two moves.

Find checkmate in one move.

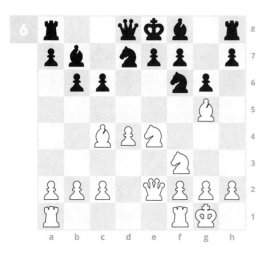

Find checkmate in one move.

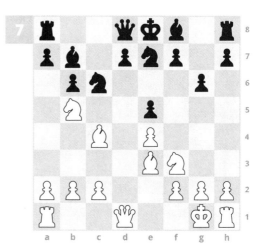

Find checkmate in one move.

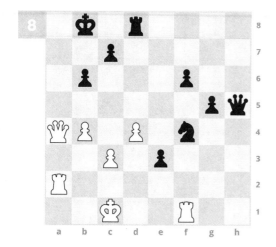

8

Find checkmate in one move.

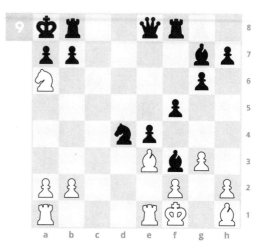

9

Find checkmate in one move.

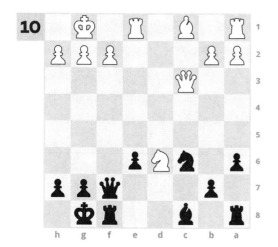

10

True or False: Black can checkmate in three moves.

11

True or False: White can checkmate in two moves by sacrificing the queen.

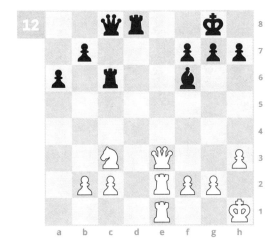

Find checkmate in three moves.

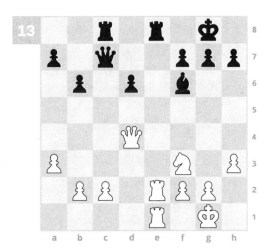

True or False: Rook captures rook on e8 will lead to checkmate.

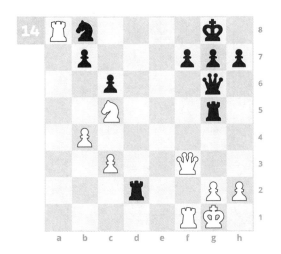

True or False: The best move is queen captures pawn on f7.

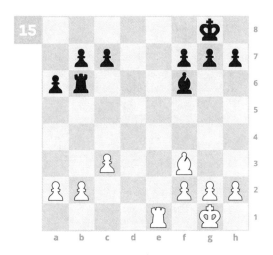

Find checkmate in one move.

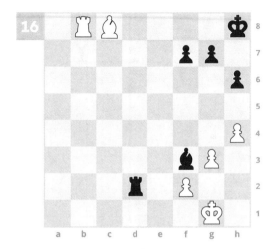

True or False: After moving the bishop to e6, white can checkmate in two moves.

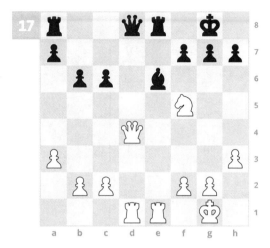

Find checkmate in one move.

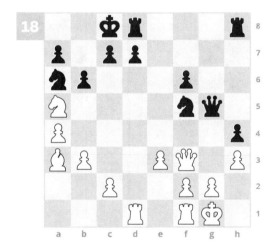

Find checkmate in one move.

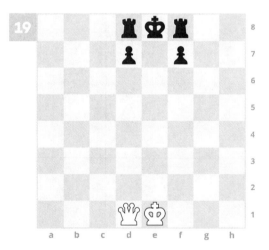

Find checkmate in one move.

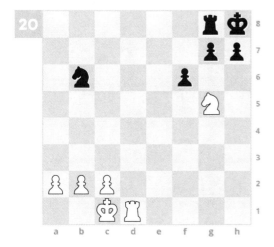

Find checkmate in one move.

True or False: There are multiple ways for white to checkmate in one move.

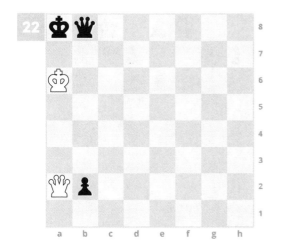

Find checkmate in two moves.

Find checkmate in one move.

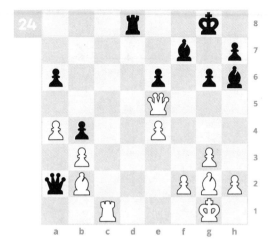

24

Find checkmate in one move.

A. Queen to g7

B. Queen to b8

C. Queen to h8

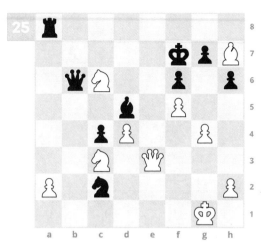

25

Find checkmate in one move.

A. Queen to e7

B. Bishop to g6

C. Queen to e6

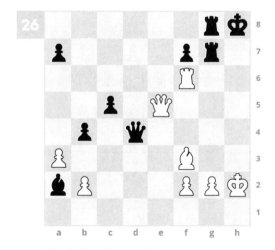

26

Find checkmate in one move.

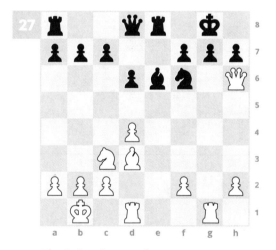

27

Find checkmate in one move.

CHAPTER 9

MIDDLE GAME STRATEGIES

In this chapter, we'll take what we've learned about attacking and defending to see how they work in middle game strategies. Don't worry if it takes time to learn how to use these strategies. Chess is all about making mistakes and learning from them!

SPACE ADVANTAGE

Players who control more space on a chessboard have a **space advantage**. It's a temporary advantage, and it's not as obvious as a material advantage. But when you control more space, you have more freedom and ability to attack. Having a space advantage also makes it tricky for your opponent to find good moves—because your pieces are everywhere!

How to get a space advantage:

- **Follow the three opening principles.** Control the center, develop your pieces, and protect your king!
- **Exchange pieces wisely.** Exchange pieces if it helps your pieces find better spots and if you have a material advantage.

Traps to avoid:

- **Don't advance too far.** If you move pieces too far from home, they might be easily captured.
- **Watch for counterattacks.** When you control a lot of space, your opponent might try to attack to switch your attention and push your pieces back.
- **Remember safety!** Make sure your pieces are protected.

DIAGRAM 9.1: White has the space advantage

True or False: White has a better space advantage.

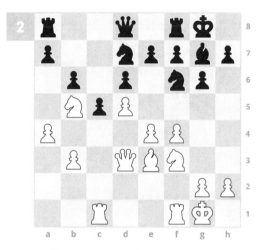

Make a move to improve your space advantage in the center.

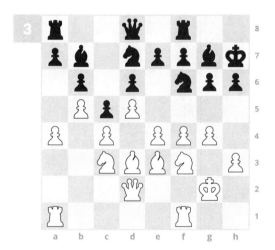

True or False: White has a better space advantage.

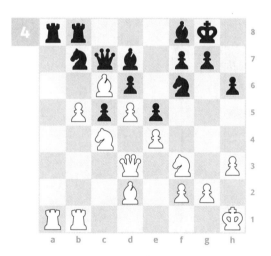

True or False: White has a better space advantage.

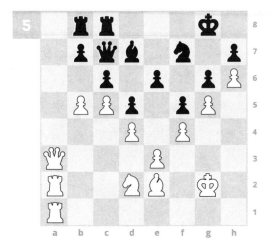

Make a move to maintain space advantage.

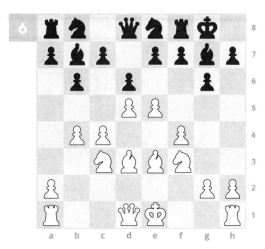

Make a move to maintain space advantage.

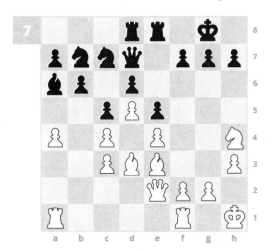

Pick the best move to maintain space advantage.

A. Queen to g4

B. Pawn to a5

C. Knight to f5

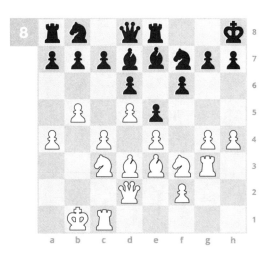

Pick the best move to maintain space advantage.

A. Pawn to g5

B. Pawn to h5

C. Pawn to c5

MATERIAL ADVANTAGE

We've explored how material advantage means having more and higher-value pieces than your opponent. As long as you can capture your opponent's pieces while protecting your own, you'll have the upper hand.

How to execute this strategy:

- **Capture your opponent's pieces.** If they leave a piece unprotected, swoop in!
- **Exchange pieces knowledgeably.** If you're ahead in material, it's usually good to exchange. Don't trade if it weakens your position.
- **Defend valuable pieces.** Place them in safe squares, and move them from danger whenever needed.

Traps to avoid:

- **Watch out for lures!** Your opponent might lure you into capturing a piece so they can capture a more valuable piece.
- **Remember your overall position.** Make sure your pieces are working together.
- **Keep an eye on your king.** Don't forget about your king's safety (see diagram 9.2).

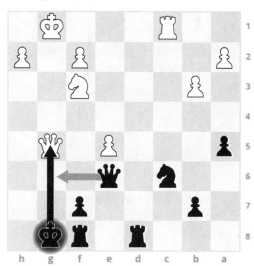

DIAGRAM 9.2: Black has an extra rook, but that doesn't mean they have the upper hand, because their king is in check. Black can stop the check by moving their queen to g6 and forcing the exchange of queens, because this move also pins the white king on g1.

Make a move to gain material advantage.

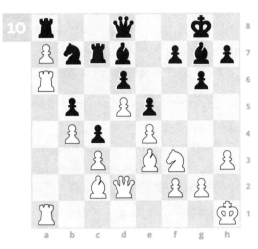

Make a move that sets you up to gain material advantage.

Make the best move to maintain material advantage.

Win a piece in two moves.

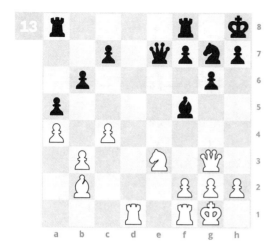

In two moves, find a way to win material.

Set up to win a piece in the next move.

Find checkmate in one move.

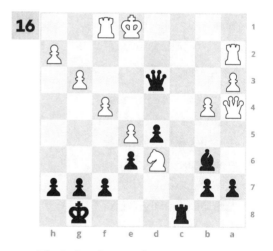

Find checkmate in two moves.

DON'T LEAVE YOUR PIECES HANGING!

As we explored earlier, hanging pieces are unprotected pieces. You can avoid hanging pieces by looking over the board and counting your pieces. Also:

- **Keep your pieces close together.** Think of a strong defense as a group of friends.
- **Avoid overextending.** Don't send your pieces too far from their "friend circle." Hanging pieces are vulnerable to attack.
- **Watch out for tricks.** Be careful of tricky moves like pins (page 80) and forks (page 73).
- **Beware of checks.** Make sure your king is defended and has an escape route.

ATTACKING HANGING PIECES

You don't want to leave *your* pieces hanging—but you *do* want to capture unprotected pieces! Here's how:

- **Threaten weaknesses.** Scan the board for hanging pieces, then move your piece where it can threaten them.
- **Choose wisely.** Aim for valuable pieces and consider risk versus reward.
- **Use teamwork.** When pieces work as a team, your attack is stronger. Consider discovered attacks (page 74) or overloading a defender (page 88).

DIAGRAM 9.3: The rook on a8 is not defended, so the queen can move to f3 and attack

17

Find the best capture.

18

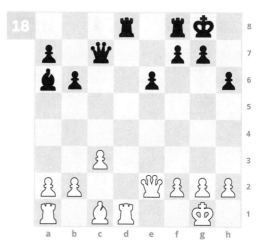

True or False: The best move is queen captures bishop on a6.

19

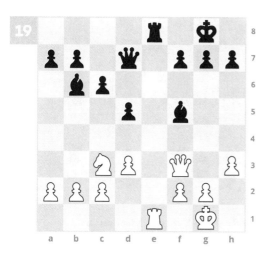

True or False: The best move is rook captures rook on e8.

20

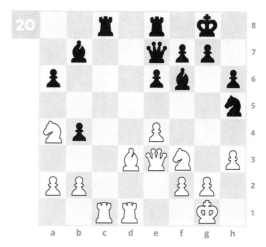

Find a way to attack the knight on h5.

Trap the bishop on a5.

A. Knight to b3

B. Knight to a4

C. Pawn to b4

Trap the knight on b4.

Find the best move to attack a hanging piece.

Find the best move to create multiple threats.

Attack a hanging piece and win material.

A. Rook to e4

B. Queen to f4

C. Rook to b4

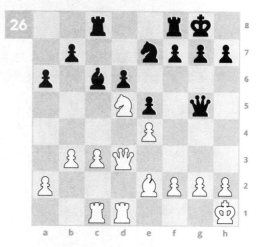

Distract the queen from defending the knight.

A. Pawn to h4

B. Pawn to f4

C. Queen to g3

Set up to attack the knight.

A. Pawn to g3

B. Bishop to e7

C. King to h2

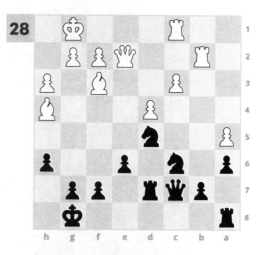

Set up to attack two major white pieces.

A. Knight to f4

B. Queen to f4

C. Knight captures pawn on d4

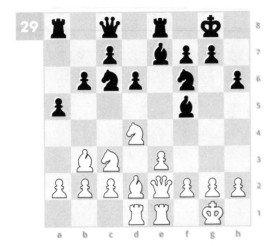

29

Find the best capture.

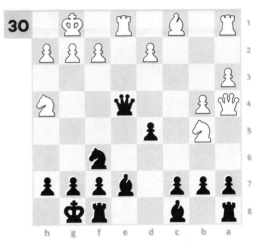

30

Find the best capture.

31

True or False: The best move is queen captures knight.

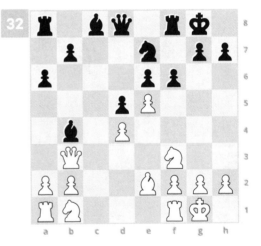

32

Find the best capture.

SACRIFICING PIECES

In chess, sacrificing a less valuable piece can lead to a big reward, like a checkmate opportunity or a more powerful piece or position. Sacrifices can also catch your opponent off guard!

How to execute this strategy:

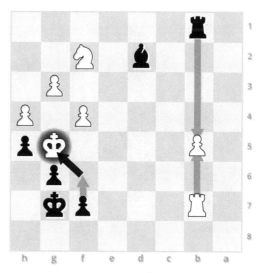

DIAGRAM 9.4: Black sacrifices its rook by capturing the pawn on b5 and checking the king on g5. White can only stop the check by capturing the rook on b5 with its rook, then black delivers a checkmate by moving the pawn to f6.

- **Calculate risk and reward.** Consider the value of the piece you're sacrificing and the possible gains. Think about how your opponent might respond.
- **Use the power of surprise.** Try not to show your strategy too early. A surprise sacrifice can make your opponent nervous, giving you an edge.
- **Look for checkmate potential.** Sacrifices are especially helpful when they open a path to the opponent's king.

Traps to avoid:

- **Don't sacrifice unnecessarily.** Have a plan and consider the advantages.
- **Don't get overwhelmed.** It's okay when sacrifices don't work—keep learning from your experiences.
- **Don't forget about your other pieces.** Make sure they're ready to jump in as needed.

33

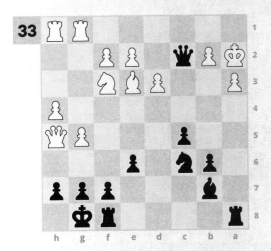

Find checkmate in two moves by sacrificing a piece.

34

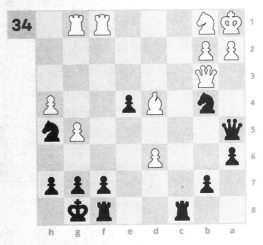

Find checkmate in two moves by sacrificing a piece.

35

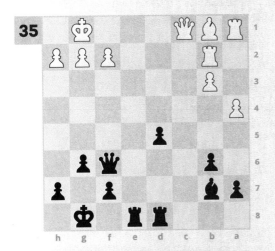

Find checkmate in two moves by sacrificing a piece.

36

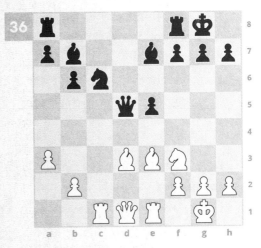

In two moves, sacrifice a minor piece to win a major piece.

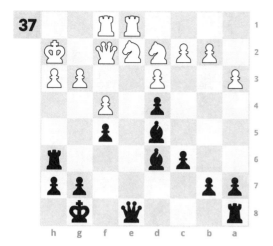

37

In two moves, sacrifice a major piece to checkmate.

38

In two moves, sacrifice your knight to checkmate.

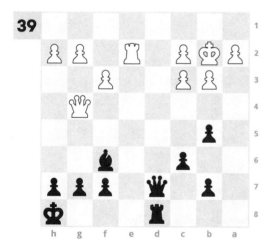

39

In two moves, find a sacrifice that will lead to checkmate.

40

In two moves, find a sacrifice that will lead to checkmate.

Sacrifice a piece to create a double attack.

A. Knight to g5

B. Knight captures pawn on f6

C. Knight to d6

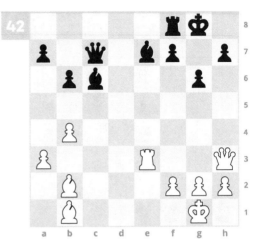

In four moves, sacrifice your queen and checkmate.

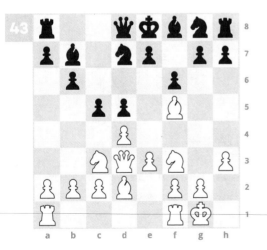

In two moves, sacrifice a piece and checkmate.

COUNTERATTACKING

Counterattacking, or responding to your opponent's threats with an attack of your own, can catch your opponent off guard, force them into defense mode, and make them rethink their moves.

How to execute this strategy:

- **Stay alert.** Pay attention to your opponent's moves and look for possible threats. If they launch a strong attack, calmly look for opportunities.
- **Look for weaknesses.** When your opponent leaves a piece unprotected or creates a weak spot, plan a counterattack to target that weakness.

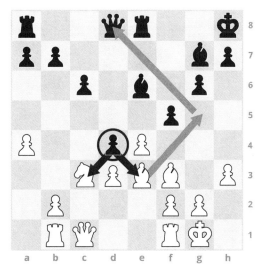

DIAGRAM 9.5: Black's pawn on d4 is forking the knight on c3 and bishop on e3. Instead of giving up one of the pieces, white will counterattack by moving the bishop to g5 and attacking the queen. Black must move its queen (for example, to d7), then the knight on c3 can run away from the pawn on d4 to e2.

- **Evaluate your moves.** Consider all the possible outcomes. Pick the move that gives you the best advantage.
- **Attack with power.** Release your counterattack with confidence!

Traps to avoid:

- **Don't rush.** Analyze the situation and make sure your counterattack is strong and effective.
- **Don't forget safety.** Always make sure your pieces are protected.
- **Watch for tricky moves.** Your opponent might set traps to attract you into a counterattack of their own.

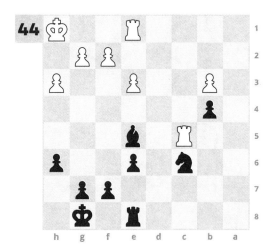

Counterattack to save the bishop on e5 and knight on c6.

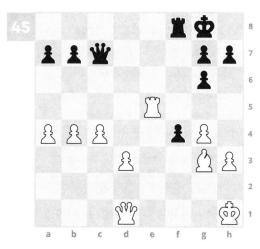

Counterattack to save the rook on e5 and bishop on g3.

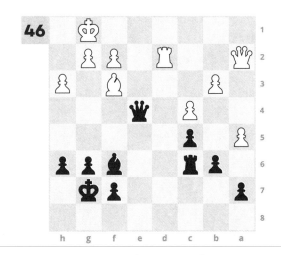

Counterattack to save the queen on e4 and rook on c6.

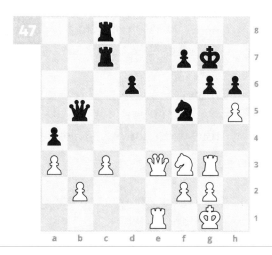

Counterattack to escape the fork from the knight on f5.

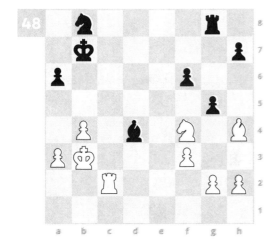

48

Counterattack to escape the fork from the pawn on g5.

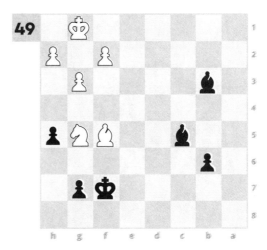

49

Escape from check and launch a counterattack.

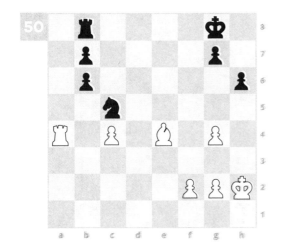

50

Counterattack to save your rook and bishop.

51

Counterattack to save your knight and bishop.

52

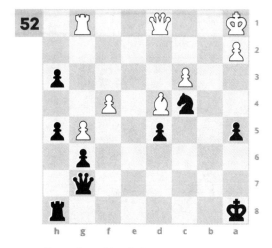

Counterattack to save your queen and rook.

53

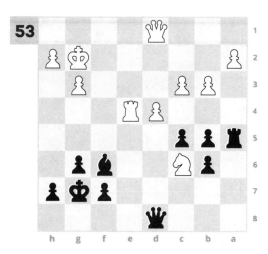

In three moves, launch a counterattack to save your queen.

54

Find a counterattack to save your knight and bishop.

55

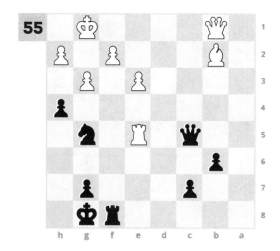

Find a counterattack to save your knight and queen.

CHAPTER 10

CHECKMATES IN THE ENDGAME

In this chapter, we'll explore powerful checkmate patterns that happen when there are fewer pieces left on the board. These checkmates require clever strategies and careful planning. Get ready to become a checkmate master!

ROOK ROLLER CHECKMATE

Also known as the two-rook checkmate, the rook roller checkmate occurs when two rooks alternate checking the opposing king until they achieve checkmate.

To execute this checkmate:

- Position two rooks on adjacent files so they can't block each other.
- Make sure no pieces are blocking the rooks' movement.
- Check the opponent's king with a rook so it moves to an adjacent square.
- Move your other rook to check the king again.
- Repeat until the king is trapped at the edge with no escape. Checkmate!

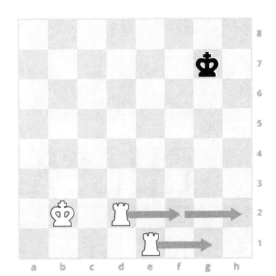

DIAGRAM 10.1: First, move the rook on d2 to f2 to block the king's escape to the f-file; the black king will move to g6.

Some things to remember:

- Don't leave your opponent's king exposed with no safe squares to move to (unless it's in check). This will lead to a half win or stalemate.
- Watch out for your opponent's king if it starts moving diagonally. If it gets dangerously close to a rook, move your rook to the other end and start again.

TWO-BISHOP CHECKMATE

In the two-bishop checkmate, two bishops work together to achieve checkmate, by using diagonal lines to trap the king into a corner.

How to execute this checkmate:

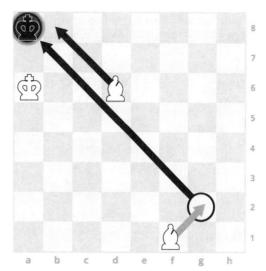

DIAGRAM 10.2: One bishop on d6 is controlling b8; the other bishop on f1 will move to g2 and checkmate.

- Move one bishop to the same diagonal as your opponent's king and check it.
- The king must move. Now move your other bishop to check the king so it must move again.
- Continue until the king has no escape squares. Checkmate!

QUEEN AND KING CHECKMATE

The queen and king checkmate (also known as queen checkmate) is an easy pattern to learn. Moving one square at a time, your queen will gradually push the king into a corner and deliver checkmate. This pattern is successful partly because a king cannot attack an opponent's queen without putting itself in check.

To execute this checkmate:

- Position your queen a knight's distance away from the opponent's king.

- Move the queen one square horizontally or diagonally at a time, and repeat until the opponent's king is at the corner.
- Bring over your king to help.
- Make sure no pieces can capture or block your queen. Then, checkmate!
- To avoid stalemate, be careful not to make the same move three times and be sure to leave the opponent's king at least one square to move to.

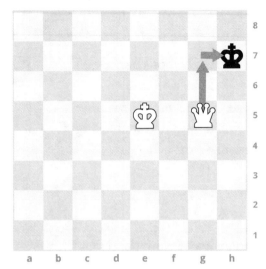

DIAGRAM 10.3: The black king is cornered on the h-file with only two safe squares (h7 and h8). Now move your king to f6 and then to f7, after which there are three checkmate options—queen to h5, queen to h4, and queen to g7.

ROOK AND KING CHECKMATE

A rook and king checkmate occurs when your rook attacks the king from the side, slowly pushing it to the edge of the board, and your king blocks their king's escape path (see diagram 10.4). It can take some time to achieve checkmate because:

- The rook must be close to the opponent's king in the same row or column.
- The opponent's king cannot escape to any safe square.
- No enemy pieces can capture or block your rooks from delivering checkmate.

To execute this checkmate:

- Push your opponent's king to the edge of the board so your rook can attack it from the side.

- Position your king in front of the opponent's king to block its path to the squares it could escape to.
- When the opponent's king is at the edge with no escape, checkmate!

One more thing: When checkmating with a rook, sometimes it requires a waiting move—a move that helps buy you time (see diagram 10.5) to finish this checkmating pattern. If you move without thinking in front of the opponent's king, and they repeat the same position three times, the game will end in a draw.

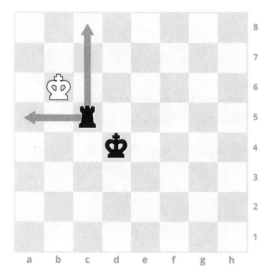

DIAGRAM 10.4: The rook on c5 has boxed in the white king and currently controls the fifth rank as well as the c-file. Now move your king to d5, forcing white to move its king to b7. Then move your rook to c6 and make the box even smaller.

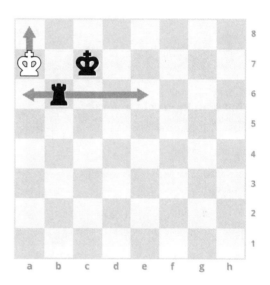

DIAGRAM 10.5: Black could deliver a check by moving rook to a6, but then it would be captured by the king. Move your rook to any other spot on the sixth rank (except for a6). The white king must move to a8 and then black will deliver a checkmate by moving rook to a6.

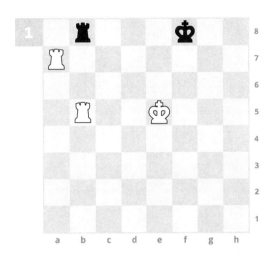

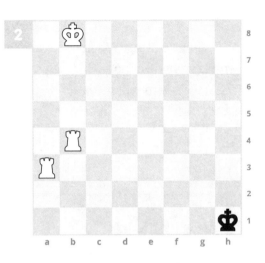

Find checkmate in one move.

What's the first move for checkmate in two moves?

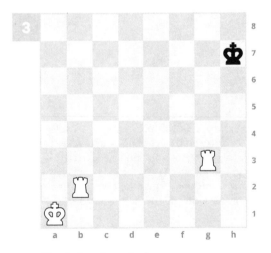

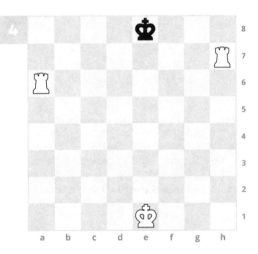

Find checkmate in one move.

Find checkmate in one move.

Find checkmate in one move.

Find checkmate in one move.

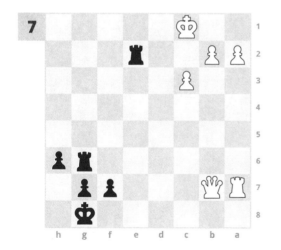

Find checkmate in one move.

Find checkmate in three moves.

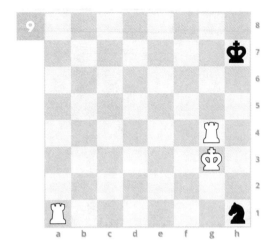

Find checkmate in one move.

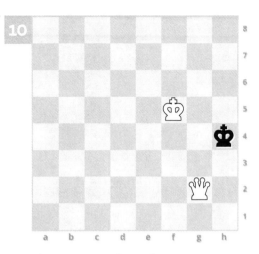

Find two possible checkmates.

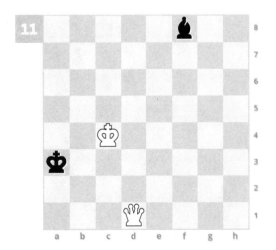

Find two possible checkmates.

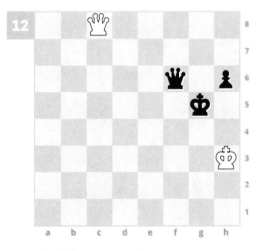

Find checkmate in one move.

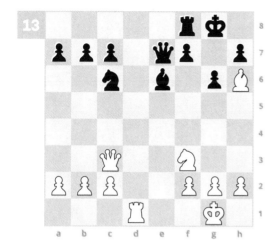

Find checkmate in one move.

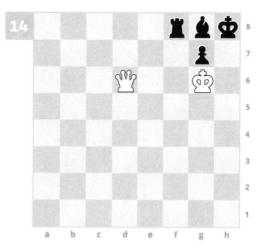

Find checkmate in two moves.

Find checkmate in one move.

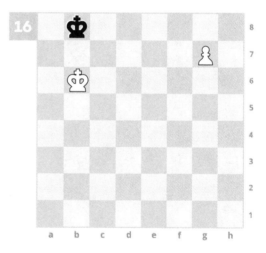

Find two possible checkmates.

17

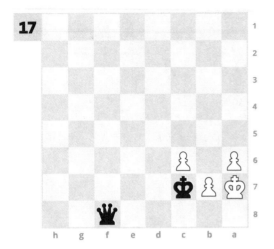

Find checkmate in one move.

18

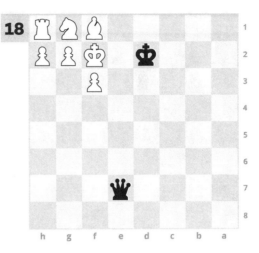

Find checkmate in one move.

19

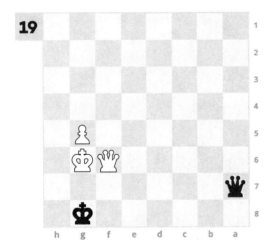

Find checkmate in one move.

20

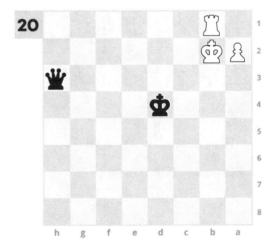

Find checkmate in one move.

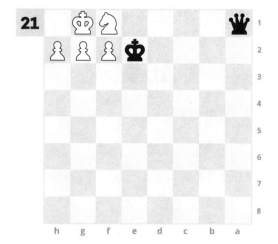

Find checkmate in one move.

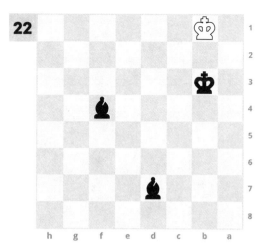

Find checkmate in two moves.

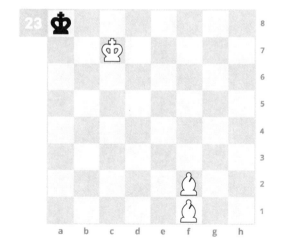

Find checkmate in one move.

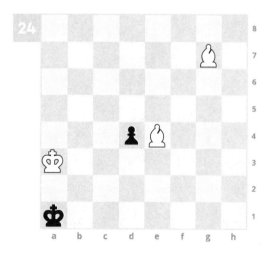

Find checkmate in one move.

25

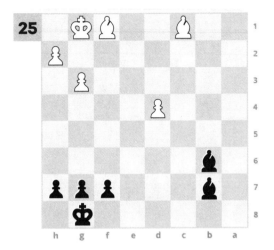

Find checkmate in two moves.

26

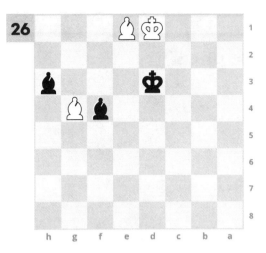

Find checkmate in one move.

27

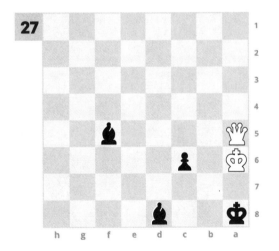

Find checkmate in one move.

28

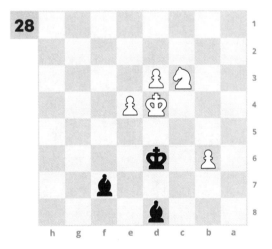

True or False: Bishop to f6 is a checkmate in one move.

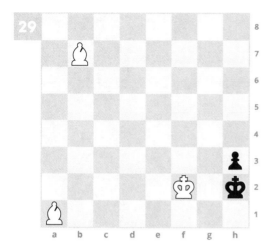

Find checkmate in one move.

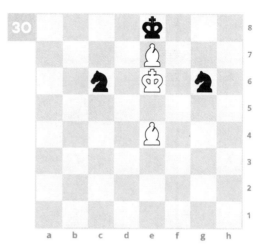

Find two possible checkmates.

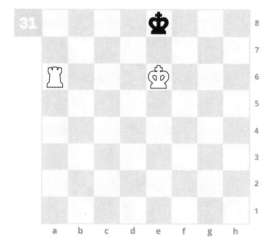

Find checkmate in one move.

Find checkmate in one move.

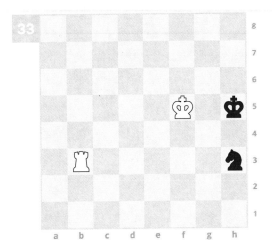

33

Find checkmate in one move.

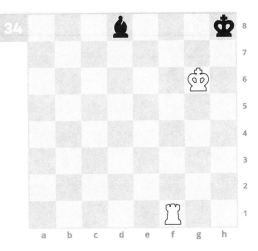

34

Find checkmate in one move.

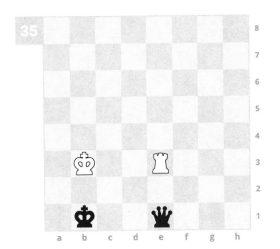

35

Find checkmate in one move.

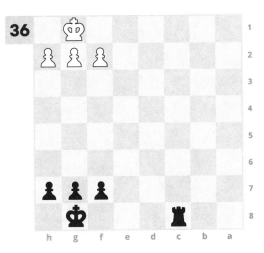

36

Find checkmate in one move.

CHAPTER 11

PLAY MORE, WIN MORE

This chapter includes a variety of exciting chess exercises designed to reinforce the concepts, tactics, and strategies discussed throughout this book. Don't worry if you get stumped by one; just move on to another one and try again later. And there's no shame in peeking at the answer key—you'll still learn something. Happy puzzling and have fun!

1

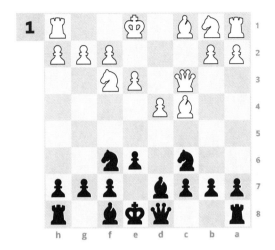

Find an absolute pin.

2

Trap white's powerful piece.

3

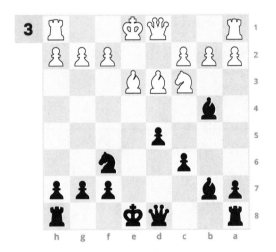

Find a fork.

4

True or False: Queen to b6 will win a bishop.

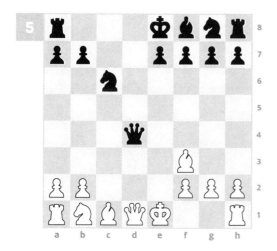

In two moves, win a powerful piece by removing the defender.

Find a discovered attack.

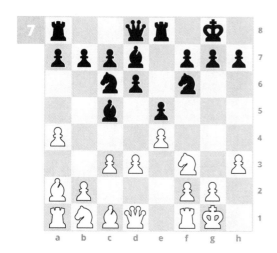

Trap the bishop on c5 in two moves.

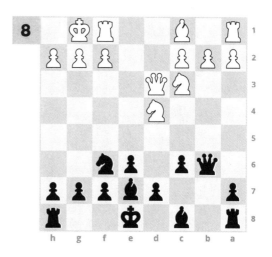

Create a skewer.

9

Trap the bishop on e5.

10

Remove the defender.

11

Find checkmate in two moves.

12

Find the best move.

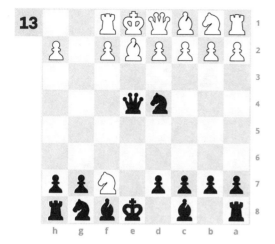

13

Find the best move.

14

Find a discovered attack.

15

Find checkmate in one move.

16

Take advantage of black's uncastled king.

17

Find a discovered attack.

18

Find the best move.

19

True or False: Rook captures pawn on f2 is a good move.

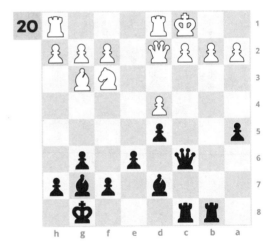

20

True or False: Pawn to e5 is your best move.

21

Find a way to attack the king.

22

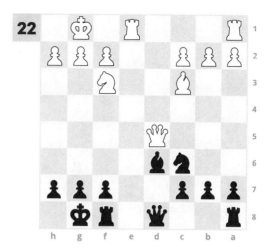

Find the best discovered attack.

23

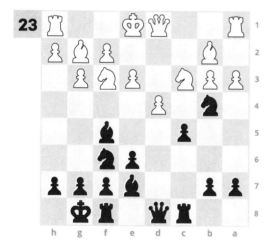

True or False: Bishop to c2 is the best move.

24

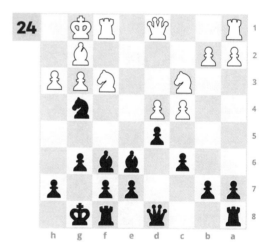

Find the best move.

25

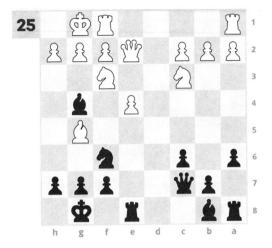

Find the best move.

26

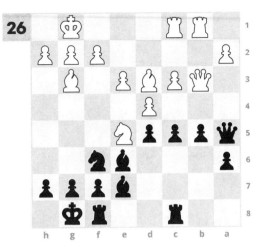

Make one move to attack two pieces.

27

Find checkmate in one move.

28

Find the best move.

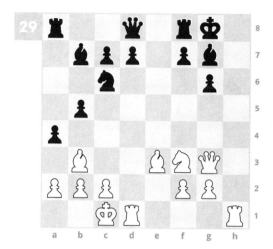

True or False: The bishop on b3 is trapped.

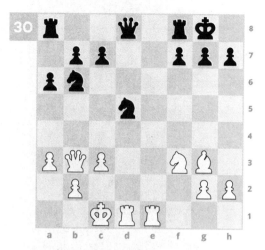

Find the best way to attack the pinned piece.

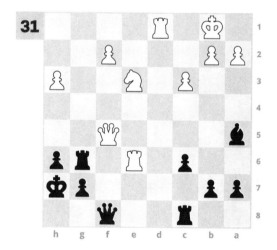

True or False: Black can stop the pin from the queen on f5.

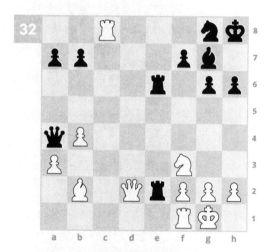

Using a pin, find checkmate in one move.

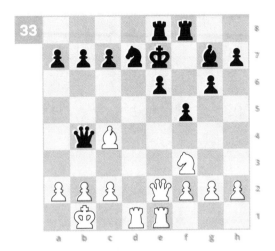

Find checkmate in two moves.

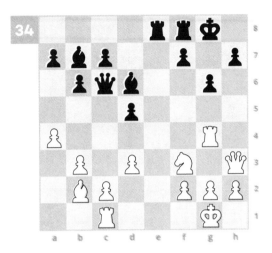

Find checkmate in three moves.

The black knight just captured a pawn on e4. Find the best move.

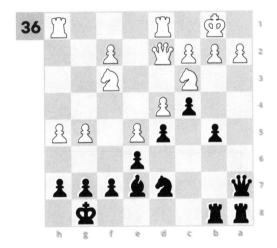

Find the best way to distract the knight from defending a2.

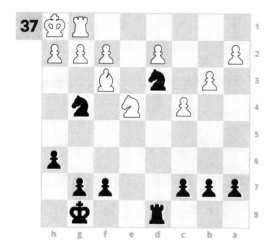

37

Find two ways to checkmate in two moves.

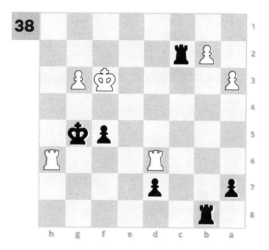

38

Find checkmate in two moves.

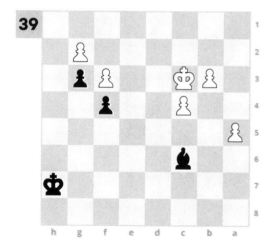

39

Find the best move after bishop captures pawn on f3, and pawn captures bishop on f3.

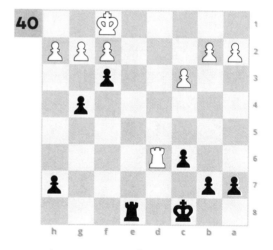

40

Distract the defender.

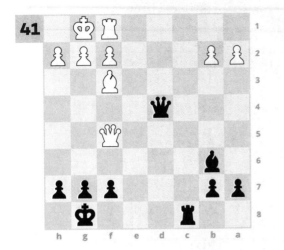

41

Find two ways to checkmate.

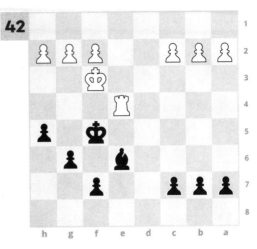

42

Find a way to pin.

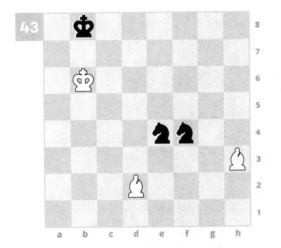

43

Find the best move.

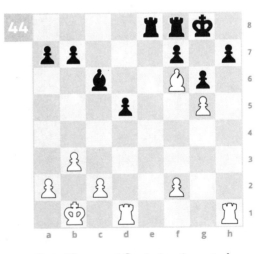

44

Sacrifice and find checkmate in three moves.

ANSWER KEY

CHAPTER 1

1. d5, because pawns can only move forward one square after their opening move.

2. No, pawns can only capture diagonally.

3. The knight on e3. Pawns capture diagonally.

4. The bishop on h7. Pawns capture diagonally.

5. Five moves, as that's how many it would need to reach the end of the board.

6. e7, f6, g5, h4, c7, b6, and a5—all the squares on the same diagonals.

7. False. The pawn is in the way.

8. Bishop captures bishop on e1, bishop captures knight on a5, and bishop captures pawn on b6.

9. d7 and d5. Moving to e4 would lead to capture by the pawn.

10. False. The white bishop is in the way.

11. C, because it is the only pawn the knight can reach.

12. False. The pawn cannot be captured by the knight, and you can only capture one piece in one move.

13. Knight on c3 to b5; knight on e6 to g5.

14. Knight on f3, rook on e5, pawn on d7, queen on c5.

15. True. Both pieces are on the same file or rank as the white rook.

16. Queen on h6, pawn on b6.

17. Rook on f1, as it has the highest point value.

18. a7, b6, b5, and d7.

19. Rook on b7. It's the highest-value piece you can capture without putting your queen in danger.

20. Bishop on d5, as the bishop is attacking your queen.

21. d4, h8, a8, a7, b6; or d4, b6, a7, a8, h8.

22. Knight on d4, as it's higher in value than the pawn.

23. Four. King to b3, king to c4, king to d5, then king captures pawn on e5; or king to c2, king to d3, king to e4, then king captures pawn on e5.

24. King to g4, king captures pawn on h3, king captures knight on g2, king to h3, then king captures bishop on h4.

CHAPTER 2

1. A. This move develops the bishop, controls the center, and attacks the pawn on f2.

2. B. White can control the center, and the bishop can possibly attack the pawn on f7.

3. C. This helps white to control the center.

4. C. This develops the knight and gives black the chance to control the center and to move the king to safety (castling).

5. B. The bishop can control the center and attack the pawn on f2, and the queen on d8 will prevent the white knight from jumping to g5.

6. C. The pawn can defend e5 and let the bishop on c8 be developed soon.

7. B. This move allows the knight to double-attack the queen on f6 and the pawn on c7.

8. C. The pawn can defend e4 and let the bishop on c1 be developed soon.

9. True. The white king is safe behind three pawns, and white's pieces have stronger control over the center. White's bishop and knight are also better developed.

10. False. This move would leave the king more vulnerable and unprotected.

11. False. Black should move a pawn to e5, to prevent the white pawn from moving to e5 to attack the knight on f6.

12. False. White shouldn't rush to capture the knight on c6. It would be better to make moves that develop pieces first, such as moving the knight to c3.

13. False. This move would leave the king vulnerable and undefended.

14. True. Both knights are controlling the center (e5 and d5), and both pawns on e4 and d4 are controlling the c5, d5, e5, and f5 squares.

15. True. The black king is behind a shield of black pawns, while the white king is undefended.

16. C. The queen will defend the pawn on f7, helping to keep the king safe.

17. B. This allows the queen to attack three pieces—king on e8, rook on h8, and bishop on c5.

18. A. This move will block the bishop from attacking the pawn on f7.

19. B. The rook is the more valuable piece.

20. B. The queen is the more valuable piece.

21. True. White can win a pawn and attack the bishop on d6.

22. C. The queen is the more valuable piece.

23. True. This will eliminate all the black pieces (except the king), so it will be easier to deliver a checkmate.

24. C. Use the knight to capture the rook, because after the black bishop captures the knight, white can win a bishop by capturing it with its rook.

25. Pawn on e5 captures pawn on d6.

26. B. The rook is worth more points than the bishop.

27. C. Although the black rook will capture the white queen after this move, you open the door for your bishop to threaten the rook on f7 and king on g8.

28. B. This way white gains a material advantage.

29. The rook on e7.

30. The queen on g4.

31. The pawn on e5. This pawn is defended twice (by the bishop on d6 and queen on e7), but it is attacked three times (by the pawn on f4, knight on f3, and rook on e1).

32. Knight captures queen on c6. The queen is the most powerful, and you can check the king.

CHAPTER 3

1. C. This move lets you control the center.

2. False. It is best to keep the pawn on d4 so it can control the center.

3. B. This is the best move to get full control of the central squares.

4. C. This move helps black control the central squares and opens up a path for the bishop on f8 to attack the white pawn on c5.

5. B. This way the pawn controls f4 and d4, and the bishop on c8 can be developed to g4.

6. A. So the pawn can control the center.

7. B. This way the knight will be able to control the center, attack e5, and defend the king.

8. A. This way white can develop the knight and control d5.

9. A. This way black can control the center, keep the king safer, and attack the pawn on f2.

10. C. This way the knight on d2 can defend the knight on f3 from the bishop on g4.

11. B. The black bishop can develop and check the white king.

12. True. Because the white king has moved to f1.

13. False. White can't castle kingside because the queen on h3 is controlling f1 and can't castle queenside because the rook on d8 is controlling the d-file.

14. True. Although the black rook has control of the b-file, white can castle queenside without the white king crossing the b-file.

15. True. The black bishop on c4 is controlling f1, preventing white from castling kingside.

16. King to g8 and rook to f8.

CHAPTER 4

1. A. Double check from the bishop and the rook on d2.

2. B. Double check from the knight on h6 and the bishop on c4.

3. B. The knight on e7 will check the king on g8 and attack the rook on c8; the queen on c4 will also check the king.

4. B. The bishop on b2 will attack the queen on a3, and the queen on e2 will check the king on e8.

5. C. This allows the rook on a1 to check the king, and the knight on e3 will attack the queen on f5.

6. B. This allows the knight on f6 to check the king, and the bishop on g2 will attack the queen on b7.

7. B. This allows the bishop to check the king on h8 and allows the rook on h4 to attack the queen on b4.

8. C. This allows the rook to check the king on g1 and the bishop on g7 to attack the queen on b2.

9. Knight to g6. This will block the check from the queen on h7 and allows you to check their king.

10. Bishop to e4 sets up an attack on the rook on b1 and allows the rook on b8 to check the white king.

11. Knight to b5 will block the check from the rook on b2 and allows you to check their white king.

12. True. This allows the rook on f1 to check the black king and sets up an attack from the bishop to the queen on b6.

13. B. This removes the attacker and escapes check.

14. B. This removes the attacker and escapes check.

15. Pawn to d5 will block the check from the bishop on b7 and save the white pawn from being captured by the black pawn on the next move.

16. B. If you move the queen to d7, you will lose your queen (a bishop exchange is preferable).

17. B. This move allows the knight to be defended by the pawn on c3. The other moves leave you vulnerable to capture.

18. B. If you choose A, then the bishop could capture your rook on a8.

19. False. The white king is in check from the pawn on h2.

20. Rook captures bishop on f4.

21. B. This is the only way to block the check and defend the bishop on a3. The other options would lose the bishop on a3.

22. C. This is the only way to block the check from the rook on f8 without losing the rook on e1.

23. C. This is the only way to escape from the check without losing pieces.

24. False. The black king on g7 is in check from the bishop on d4.

CHAPTER 5

1. False. The pawn on c7 is a passed pawn.

2. Pawns on g4 and b7. Neither pawn can be stopped by black pawns.

3. True. The pawn on d3 is a backward pawn and can be easily attacked by black pieces.

4. The pawn on d4. It is not supported by any other white pawns.

5. B. It is not supported by any black pawns and has no opportunity to advance.

6. False, the two pawns are on the same rank not the same file.

7. Three moves.

8. True. Black has a better pawn shield next to its king. The white pawn on g3 leaves a lot of light-square weaknesses, such as h3, g2, and f3.

9. True. The pawn on f3 is defended by the pawn on g2.

10. True. If there were no pawn on g3, black would deliver a checkmate on g2.

11. False. They are a pawn shield.

12. True. Pawns on a4, b4, and c4 are standing next to each other and supporting each other.

13. False. The pawns on f2 and f4 are the only doubled pawns.

14. The pawn on h6.

15. True. There are no white pawns on the neighboring files. It is also a passed pawn.

16. C. Pawn to b4 will prevent the white pawn on a2 from moving forward. This way black will be able to advance another pawn to a4 easily.

17. Pawn moves to a6 and captures the black pawn en passant.

18. Pawn on c4 captures pawn on b4 by moving to b3 (en passant).

19. Pawn moves to h3 and captures the white pawn en passant.

20. False. We can never promote a pawn to a king.

21. True. Either a queen or a rook can deliver a checkmate.

22. C. This will deliver a checkmate immediately because the king won't have any squares to escape to.

CHAPTER 6

1. Pawn to f4 to attack the king and the rook.

2. Pawn to e1, promote to knight.

3. Queen to e5 to attack the black king on e8 and the rook on b2.

4. Pawn to c5 to attack the king on b6 and the queen on d6.

5. Bishop to e5. This targets both undefended rooks.

6. Pawn to b4. This uses a pawn to target two powerful pieces—the rook and the knight.

7. C. This will attack the knight on g4 and bishop on e4.

8. B. This will attack the bishop on b7 and bishop on g7.

9. Pawn to d8, promote to knight. This checks the king on b7 and attacks the queen on e6.

10. Pawn to b4 to attack the knight on c3 and the knight on a3.

11. B. The knight on e3 will attack the rook on g4, and the rook on d1 will attack the queen on d8.

12. B. Bishop to b2 will attack the rook on f6, and the rook on a1 will attack the queen on a8.

13. C. Knight to e4 will double-attack the queen on g3 and the rook on d2.

14. B. Knight to h4 will double check the king on g2 and attack the queen on f5.

15. Bishop captures pawn on g7, checks the king on h8, and attacks the queen on b4, winning it on the next move.

16. Bishop captures pawn on h2, which checks the king on g1, and the queen on d7 will attack the queen on d5.

17. Pawn to c5 will check the king on a6 with the bishop on d3, and the pawn on c5 will attack the black rook on b6.

18. Knight to d3 checks the king. The knight will be defended by the queen on d7, while the rook on e8 will attack the queen on e4.

19. Rook to e3 checks the king, while the queen on c2 will attack the black queen on h7. After the king runs away from the check, white will capture the black queen on h7.

20. Rook to c8 will be a double check from the queen on b3 and the rook on c8. After the king runs away to h7, white will capture the black queen on a8.

21. B. Bishop to b5 will create an absolute pin by attacking the queen on d7 and king on e8.

22. A. Bishop to c4 will create an absolute pin by attacking the rook on d5 and king on g8.

23. The knight on f3 is pinned by the bishop on b7. The black queen can capture the bishop on g5 because the defending knight on f3 is pinned by the bishop.

24. Pawn to b5 will attack the pinned knight (pinned by the bishop on g2). Black will capture on b5, and white will recapture on b5, still putting pressure on the pinned piece.

25. C. Rook to c1 will put extra pressure on the pinned knight on c5. If black keeps the knight on c5, it will be captured by the queen on c2. And if the black queen then captures the white queen, the white rook will capture the black queen. If the knight moves away from c5, white will capture the queen on c8.

26. A. Rook to f2 will create an absolute pin with the queen on e2 and the king on c2.

27. A. Bishop to c3 will create an absolute pin with the knight on e5 and the king on g7.

28. C. Queen captures knight on h5, check. Black cannot capture the queen back because the bishop on c2 is pinning the pawn on g6 and king on h7.

29. B. Bishop captures pawn on h4, check. The bishop skewers the king on f6 and rook on d8.

30. A. Rook to d1, check. The rook will skewer the king on d7 and queen on d8.

31. B. Rook to d1 will skewer the queen on d5 and knight on d7.

32. C. The bishop on d3 will skewer the rook on f5 and rook on g6. While A creates a skewer, the pawn on h5 is defended, making it not the best option.

33. A. Bishop to b6 will skewer the queen on c7 and rook on d8.

34. C. Bishop to d5 will skewer the king on e4 and queen on g2.

35. B. Bishop to h6 will skewer the king on g7 and rook on f8.

36. C. Bishop to c4 will skewer the king on e6 and rook on g8.

37. C. Rook to h1 will skewer the king on f1 and queen on d1.

38. C. Queen to h7 will skewer the king on c2 and queen on b1.

CHAPTER 7

1. Bishop captures knight on b6, check; king captures back; rook captures bishop on d5.

2. Queen captures queen on c2, knight captures back; rook captures rook on a4.

3. Bishop captures knight on d5, check; pawn captures bishop on d5; queen captures queen on f4, check.

4. Queen captures queen on c4, check; pawn captures queen on c4; rook captures rook on e2.

5. Bishop captures knight on d5, queen captures queen on b7, bishop captures queen on b7.

6. Queen captures queen on g7, check; king captures queen on g7; bishop captures knight on e5, check.

7. Bishop captures knight on d5.

8. Knight captures bishop on g4, check; pawn captures knight on g4; rook captures rook on d7.

9. Bishop captures knight on e3, check.

10. Bishop captures knight on e3, check.

11. Bishop captures knight on f5, check.

12. Pawn to b6.

13. Rook to a1, check; bishop to g1; queen captures queen on b6.

14. Pawn to f6, check.

15. Rook to f1, check; king to g8; rook captures rook on e8, check.

16. Rook to e8 (pinning the queen on f8 and king on g8); queen captures rook on e8; queen to g7, checkmate.

17. Pawn to c4.

18. Bishop to a7, check.

19. Pawn to g5, knight to h5; rook captures knight on d5.

20. Pawn to d5; knight to e7; knight captures bishop on b4.

21. Pawn to d4; bishop to f6; bishop captures knight on f4.

22. Pawn to h7, check.

23. Pawn captures pawn on f2, check.

CHAPTER 8

1. C. Knight to f2 will be a checkmate because the queen on g1 is pinned by the rook on d1.

2. B. Knight to f4 will be a checkmate because the knight will control g6 (the escape square for the king).

3. C. Knight to b6 will be a checkmate because the pawn on a7 is pinned by the rook on a1.

4. Queen to g8; rook captures queen on g8; knight to f7 will be a smothered checkmate.

5. Knight to f6 will be a checkmate because the rook is pinning the bishop on g7 and the king on h7 can't run away to g6 because of the pawn on h5.

6. Knight to d6 will be a checkmate because the pawn on e7 is pinned by the queen on e2.

7. Knight to d6 will be a smothered checkmate.

8. Queen to a8, checkmate.

9. Knight to c7 will be a smothered checkmate.

10. True. Queen captures pawn on f2, check; king to h1; queen to f1, check; rook captures queen on f1; rook to f1, checkmate.

11. True. Queen captures rook on f8, check; king captures queen on f8; rook to e8, checkmate.

12. 1. Queen to e8, check; rook captures queen on e8. 2. Rook captures rook on e8, check; queen captures rook on e8. 3. Rook captures queen on e8, checkmate.

13. True. Rook captures rook on e8, check; rook captures rook on e8; rook captures rook on e8, checkmate.

14. False. The best move is rook captures knight on b8, check; rook to d8; rook captures rook on d8, checkmate.

15. Rook to e8, checkmate.

16. False. After the bishop moves to e6, the king will run away to h7. The best move is bishop to f5, check; rook to d8; rook captures rook on d8, checkmate.

17. Queen captures pawn on g7, checkmate.

18. Queen to b7, checkmate.

19. Queen to e2, checkmate.

20. Knight to f7 leaves the black king with no escape (a smothered checkmate).

21. False. The only way to checkmate is queen captures pawn on h7, checkmate.

22. 1. Queen to d5, check; queen to b7. 2. Queen captures queen on b7, checkmate.

23. Queen to g7, checkmate.

24. C. Queen to h8, checkmate, because the bishop on b2 is defending the white queen.

25. A. Queen to e7, checkmate, because the knight on c6 is defending the white queen.

26. Rook to h6, checkmate.

27. Queen captures pawn on g7. This works because the rook on g1 is defending it.

CHAPTER 9

1. True. The white pawns on d4 and e5 are controlling the major squares in the center.

2. Pawn to e5. This helps you attack the knight on f6 and pawn on d6.

3. True. Most of the black pieces are on the sixth, seventh, and eighth ranks, while the white pawns are controlling central squares.

4. True. White's position is better because most of its pieces are focused on the kingside, and its pawns on d5 and e4 are controlling the center.

5. Pawn to b6 will attack the queen on c7, limit black's position, and control more dark squares, like a7 and c7.

6. Queen to d2 allows white to make more strategic moves to protect its knight and move its rook out. Moving any of the pawns further out would make them more vulnerable.

7. C. Knight to f5 will control d6, e7, g7, and h6.

8. A. This move will attack f6, so if black captures the pawn on g5, white will recapture on g5 with the pawn on h4, opening the h-file and controlling h6 and f6.

9. Pawn to e5 to attack the knight on f6 and bishop on d6, winning one of them.

10. Bishop to b6 will pin the rook and the queen.

11. Pawn captures pawn on e4 allows you to attack the pinned knight on f3.

12. 1. Rook to e1. 2. Rook captures queen on e4.

13. 1. Knight captures bishop on f5; pawn captures knight on f5. 2. Queen captures knight on g7, checkmate.

14. Bishop to b3 means the knight on c2 will be trapped, facing capture anywhere it tries to move.

15. Rook captures pawn on a2 means the king won't be able to run away to b5 (the knight on c7 is controlling it).

16. 1. Rook to c1, check; white queen to d1. 2. Rook or queen captures queen on d1, checkmate.

17. Queen captures bishop on b5. If the white queen then takes the bishop on b7, your queen can win the knight on e2.

18. False. After the queen captures bishop on a6, the black rook will capture the rook on d1.

19. True. The best move will be rook captures rook on e8, check; queen captures it back; queen captures bishop on f5.

20. Pawn to g4.

21. C. This move means the bishop on a5 will have no available squares to go to and white can capture it, only losing one pawn in the process.

22. Queen to b3. The black knight won't have any safe squares to run away to.

23. Bishop to g2.

24. Queen to e5 will threaten checkmate on h2 and it will attack the knight on b5.

25. C. Rook to b4 will double-attack the bishop on a4 and bishop on h4.

26. C. This move means black will have to react. If queen captures queen on g3, knight captures knight on e7, check; king to h8; and pawn on h2 captures queen on g3.

27. B. This will attack the rook on d8 and knight on h4. If rook captures bishop on e7, white rook captures rook on d8, check. If rook captures rook on d1, white will use the bishop on e2 to capture rook on d1.

28. B. This will attack the rook on c1 and bishop on h4.

29. Knight captures knight on c6. This is the only undefended piece.

30. Queen captures rook on e1, checkmate.

31. False. After the queen captures the knight on e6, white will move their bishop to c4. The best move is rook to f6.

32. Queen captures bishop on b4.

33. 1. Rook captures pawn on a3, check; king captures rook on a3. 2. Rook to a8, checkmate.

34. 1. Queen captures pawn on a2, check; white queen captures queen on a2. 2. Knight to c2, checkmate.

35. 1. Queen captures rook on b2; white queen captures queen on b2. 2. Rook to e1, checkmate.

36. 1. Bishop captures pawn on h7, check; black king captures bishop on h7. 2. Queen captures queen on d5.

37. 1. Rook captures pawn on h3, check; white king captures rook on h3. 2. Queen to h5, checkmate; or 1. Rook captures pawn on h3, check; white king to g1. 2. Rook to h1, checkmate.

38. 1. Knight to f6; black pawn captures knight on f6. 2. Queen captures pawn on h7, checkmate; or 1. Knight to f6; black knight captures queen on d3. 2. Rook captures pawn on h7, checkmate.

39. 1. Bishop captures pawn on c3; king captures bishop at c3. 2. Queen to d4, checkmate.

40. 1. Bishop captures pawn on g2, check; king captures bishop on g2. 2. Knight to f4, checkmate.

41. B. This will threaten checkmate on h7 (from the queen on h6, knight on f6, and bishop on c2) and double-attack the rooks on d7 and g8.

42. 1. Queen captures pawn on h7; king captures queen on h7. 2. Rook to h3, check; bishop to h4. 3. Rook captures bishop on h4, check; king to g8. 4. Rook to h8, checkmate.

43. 1. Bishop to g6; pawn captures bishop on g6. 2. Queen captures pawn on g6, checkmate.

44. Bishop to c3. This move attacks the white rook protecting the king.

45. Rook to c5 will attack the queen (with protection from the pawn on b4), and it will give the bishop time to run away to f2.

46. Queen to e1, check.

47. Knight to d4 will attack the queen on b5 and knight on f5, stopping the fork.

48. Knight to e6 or knight to e2.

49. King to f6. This attacks both the bishop and the knight.

50. Bishop to d5, check.

51. The best move is bishop to b5, so you can attack the undefended rook on e8 and gain time to save the knight on h4.

52. Queen to b7 will run away from the skewer (the bishop on d4 attacking both the queen on g7 and rook on h8). This will create a checkmate threat on b2 and allow you to save your rook on h8.

53. 1. Queen to d5; knight captures rook on a5. 2. Queen captures rook on e4, check; king to g1. 3. Pawn captures knight on a5.

54. Knight to d5 will help you save your bishop on e3. Black will need to save their queen by moving it to d8. Then move white bishop to f4 or d2 so the pawn on d4 can't capture it.

55. Knight to f3, check. This creates a double attack on the king on g1 and rook to e5. After the king runs away to a safe square (g2, h1, or f1), your knight on f3 can capture the rook on e5.

CHAPTER 10

1. Rook captures rook on b8, checkmate.

2. Rook to b2 or rook to a2, followed by rook to a1 or rook to b1, checkmate.

3. Rook to h2, checkmate.

4. Rook to a8, checkmate.

5. Rook captures pawn on a2, checkmate.

6. Rook captures pawn on h2, checkmate.

7. Rook to g1, checkmate.

8. 1. Rook to b8, check; black bishop to c8. 2. Rook captures bishop on c8, check; black bishop to d8. 3. Rook captures bishop on d8, checkmate.

9. Rook captures knight on h1, checkmate.

10. Queen to h2, checkmate, and queen to g4, checkmate.

11. Queen to b3, checkmate, and queen to a1, checkmate.

12. Queen to g4, checkmate.

13. Queen to g7, checkmate.

14. 1. Queen to h2, check; bishop to h7. 2. Queen captures bishop on h7, checkmate.

15. Queen captures pawn on g7, checkmate, because the bishop on b2 is defending it.

16. Pawn to g8, promotion to queen or rook, checkmate.

17. Queen to b8, checkmate.

18. Queen to e1, checkmate.

19. Queen to h7, checkmate, so the king can't run away to f5.

20. Queen to c3, checkmate.

21. Queen captures knight on f1, checkmate.

22. 1. Bishop to f5, check; king to a1. 2. Bishop to e5, checkmate.

23. Bishop to g2, checkmate.

24. Bishop captures pawn on d4, checkmate.

25. 1. Bishop captures pawn on d4, check; bishop to e3. 2. Bishop captures bishop on e3, checkmate.

26. Bishop captures bishop on g4, checkmate.

27. Bishop to c8 will be a checkmate, because the bishop on d8 is controlling the b6 square, and the pawn on c6 is controlling b5.

28. False. The king will be able to run away to e3. The checkmate will be after bishop captures pawn on b6.

29. Bishop to e5, checkmate.

30. Bishop captures knight on g6, checkmate, and bishop captures knight on c6, checkmate.

31. Rook to a8, checkmate.

32. Rook to a1, checkmate.

33. Rook captures knight on h3, checkmate.

34. Rook to f8, checkmate.

35. Rook captures queen on e1, checkmate.

36. Rook to c1, checkmate.

CHAPTER 11

1. Bishop to b4 is an absolute pin, pinning the queen on c3 and king on e1 because the queen wouldn't be able to run away without exposing the king to check.

2. Knight to h5 means the queen on g3 will have no squares to move to without being captured.

3. Pawn to d4 will fork the bishop on e3 and the knight on c3.

4. False. The bishop still can run away to c4 or a4. The best move is queen to a5 so it can check the king on e1 and attack the undefended bishop on b5.

5. 1. Bishop captures knight on c6, check; pawn captures bishop on c6. 2. Queen captures queen on d4, check.

6. 1. Bishop to b5, check; king to d8. 2. Queen captures queen on d4.

7. Pawn to b4; bishop to b6. Pawn to a5 traps the bishop.

8. Bishop to a6 will attack both the queen on d3 and the rook on f1. The queen can run away to g3, but then white will still lose its rook to your bishop.

9. Pawn to f6; bishop to f4. Pawn to g5; bishop to g3. Pawn to h4.

10. Queen captures bishop on e5 (it is defending h2, even though there is a black pawn on g3).

11. 1. Bishop captures pawn on f2, check; king to e2. 2. Bishop to g4, checkmate.

12. Queen to c1, checkmate.

13. Knight to f3, checkmate.

14. Pawn to e5 will attack the knight on f6 and the rook on a8. After the knight escapes to g8, your bishop on g2 can capture the rook on a8.

15. Queen captures pawn on h7, checkmate.

16. Knight captures pawn onf7, forking the king on d8 and the rook on h8.

17. Pawn to d5 will attack the knight on c6 and allow the bishop on e3 to attack the queen on b6. After the black queen moves to a5 and checks your king on e1, you could move your bishop to d2 to block the check, and then use your pawn on d5 to capture the black knight next.

18. Queen to h5, check; pawn to g6 (the only way to stop the check). Pawn on f5 captures pawn on g6; pawn on h7 captures pawn on g6. Queen captures pawn on g6, checkmate.

19. True. The pawn on f2 is attacked three times with both rooks (f8 and f7) and the queen on c5, and only defended with the king on g1 and rook on f1. So it is a good idea to capture the weak pawn on f2.

20. False. Your best move is to defend the rook on b8 by moving it to b7.

21. Bishop captures pawn on h2 acts as a sacrifice. Once the king captures the bishop, both queen to h4 and knight to g4 would check the king on h2.

22. Bishop captures pawn on h2 attacks the king on g1 and reveals an attack on the undefended queen on d5.

23. False. Knight to c2 will be best because it will attack the king on e1 and rook on a1.

24. Knight to e3 will fork the rook on f1 and queen on d1.

25. Bishop captures knight on f3 followed with queen captures pawn on h2, checkmate.

26. Pawn to c4 will attack the queen on b3 and the bishop on d3. After the queen escapes, your pawn can capture the bishop.

27. Knight captures pawn on c2, checkmate.

28. Knight to f6 will check the king on g8, and attack the queen on h5 and the bishop on g4. After the king escapes check, the knight can capture the queen.

29. False. The bishop is not trapped, it can move to d5.

30. Pawn to c4 will attack the pinned knight on d5.

31. True. The black queen can capture white's queen on f5, eliminating the pin.

32. Queen captures pawn on h6 will deliver a checkmate because the bishop on g7 and knight on g8 are pinned and unable to capture it back on h6.

33. 1. Queen captures pawn on e6; king to d8. 2. Queen captures knight on d7, checkmate.

34. 1. Queen captures pawn on h7; king captures queen on h7. 2. Rook to h4; king to g8. 3. Rook to h8, checkmate.

35. Bishop captures queen on d8.

36. Pawn to b4 attacks the knight on c3, and after the knight runs away to e2, black can capture the pawn on a2 and later deliver a checkmate on a1.

37. Either of the black knights can capture on f2, leading to checkmate. For example, knight on g4 captures pawn on f2; white knight captures black knight on f2. 2. Black knight captures white knight on f2, checkmate.

38. 1. Rook on b8 to b3, check; rook to d3 2. Rook captures rook on d3, checkmate.

39. Pawn to g2, promotion to queen in the next move on g1.

40. Rook to e1, check, followed by pawn captures pawn on g2 and promotion on g1.

41. 1. Queen captures pawn on f2, check; rook captures queen on f2. 2. Rook to c1, check; bishop to d1. 3. Rook captures bishop on d1, checkmate. *Or* 1. Queen captures pawn on f2, check; king to h1. 2. Queen captures rook on f1, checkmate.

42. Bishop to d5.

43. Bishop captures knight on f4, check.

44. 1. Rook captures pawn on h7; king captures rook on h7. 2. Rook to h1, check; king to g8. 3. Rook to h8, checkmate.

INDEX

Page numbers in italics indicate diagrams.

R

ranks, *9*, 9–10, *10*
rooks, 9
    captures by, 14
    captures of, 74, *74*, 88, *88*
    castling, 41, *42*, 42–43, *43*
    developing, 41
    fork, 74
    movement, 14, *14*
    notation for, 10
    point value, 14
    rook and king checkmate with, 132–33, *133*
    rook roller checkmate with, 130, *130*
    strengths and weaknesses, 14

S

sacrificing pieces, 121, *121*
skewers, 83, *83*
smothered checkmate, *98*, 99
space advantage, 110, *110*
squares, notation for, 10, *10*
stages, of game, 24–25
stalemate, 100
strategy
    active pieces, 32, *32*
    attacking hanging pieces, 116, *116*
    centering, 40, *40*
    controlling middle of board, 25
    counterattacking, 125, *125*
    exchanges, 34, *34*
    gaining material advantage, 32, 34, 113, *113*
    keeping king safe, 25–26, *26*, 40, 42
    middle game, 109–10, 113, 116, 121, 125
    of three phases, 24–25

T

threefold repetition, 100
two-bishop checkmate, 131, *131*
two-rook checkmate, 130, *130*

W

winning, response to, 24

ACKNOWLEDGMENTS

Creating a book has proven to be more challenging than I initially anticipated, yet it has brought me greater satisfaction than I could have ever envisioned. My gratitude goes out to my close friends for all their support and advice as I wrote this book, especially David Buric, Jennifer Sensakovic, and Carey Fan. And of course, my deepest thanks to all my chess students for their support and for always putting a smile on my face!

ABOUT THE AUTHOR

 **VIKTORIA NI** has been playing and studying chess for over 25 years. She was first taught chess by her mother, Polina, at the age of seven and was later trained by Grandmaster Janis Klovans. In 2010, Viktoria achieved the title of Woman International Master (WIM). Viktoria is a two-time Latvian women's champion of rapid chess (2004 and 2005), a national Latvian girls' U18 youth champion (2009), and the U18 girls European rapid chess champion (2009). Viktoria represented the US as part of the Women's National Team in many international tournaments from 2012–2015, and was the highest-ranking U21 female chess player in the US from 2012–2013. She placed fourth in the US Women's Chess Championship twice (2012 and 2015).

In her 13-year teaching career, Viktoria has mentored thousands of students, both in person and online. She has designed chess curricula, trained other chess teachers, and run successful chess programs in New York City. Several of her students have gone on to compete at the national and international levels. Outside of chess, Viktoria enjoys traveling, reading, playing pickleball, and learning new things.

Hi, parents and caregivers,

We hope your child enjoyed *Winning Chess Exercises for Kids*. If you have any questions or concerns about this book, or have received a damaged copy, please contact customerservice@penguinrandomhouse.com. We're here and happy to help.

Also, please consider writing a review on your favorite retailer's website to let others know what you and your child thought of the book!

Sincerely,

The Zeitgeist Team